ROAD TRANSPORT RESEARCH

integrated strategies
for safety and environment

ORGANISATION FOR ECONOMIC CO-OPERATION AND DEVELOPMENT

ORGANISATION FOR ECONOMIC CO-OPERATION AND DEVELOPMENT

Pursuant to Article 1 of the Convention signed in Paris on 14th December 1960, and which came into force on 30th September 1961, the Organisation for Economic Co-operation and Development (OECD) shall promote policies designed:

- to achieve the highest sustainable economic growth and employment and a rising standard of living in Member countries, while maintaining financial stability, and thus to contribute to the development of the world economy;
- to contribute to sound economic expansion in Member as well as non-member countries in the process of economic development; and
- to contribute to the expansion of world trade on a multilateral, non-discriminatory basis in accordance with international obligations.

The original Member countries of the OECD are Austria, Belgium, Canada, Denmark, France, Germany, Greece, Iceland, Ireland, Italy, Luxembourg, the Netherlands, Norway, Portugal, Spain, Sweden, Switzerland, Turkey, the United Kingdom and the United States. The following countries became Members subsequently through accession at the dates indicated hereafter: Japan (28th April 1964), Finland (28th January 1969), Australia (7th June 1971), New Zealand (29th May 1973), Mexico (18th May 1994), the Czech Republic (21st December 1995), Hungary (7th May 1996), Poland (22nd November 1996) and the Republic of Korea (12th December 1996). The Commission of the European Communities takes part in the work of the OECD (Article 13 of the OECD Convention).

Publié en français sous le titre :
STRATÉGIES INTÉGRÉES DE SÉCURITÉ ET D'ENVIRONNEMENT

FOREWORD

The Programme centres on road and road transport research, while taking into account the impacts of intermodal aspects on the road transport system as a whole. It is geared towards a technico-economic approach to solving key road transport issues identified by Member countries. The Programme has two main fields of activity:

- International research and policy assessments of road and road transport issues to provide scientific support for decisions by Member governments and international governmental organisations;

- Technology transfer and information exchange through two databases - the International Road Research Documentation (IRRD) scheme and the International Road Traffic and Accident Database (IRTAD).

Its mission is to:

- Enhance innovative research through international co-operation and networking;

- Undertake joint policy analyses and prepare technology reviews of critical road transport issues;

- Promote the exchange of scientific and technical information in the transport sector and contribute to road technology transfer in OECD Member and non-member countries.

The scientific and technical activities concern:

- Infrastructure research;

- Road traffic and intermodal transport;

- Environment/transport interactions;

- Traffic safety research;

- Strategic research planning

ABSTRACT

IRRD N° 892068

The report was prepared by a Scientific Expert Group of the OECD formed in 1995 to study how evaluation methods and planning tools can be designed and used to give equal and co-ordinated consideration to the safety and environmental effects of road transport. The report is based on an international survey of the experience of OECD Member countries focusing on the integration of safety and environmental aspects in urban and transport planning. National strategies to tackle traffic safety and environment problems are analysed together with the national, regional and local institutional frameworks. Based on an outline of the problems and challenges included in Chapter I *Introduction*, Chapter II sets out *the potential for integration* and Chapter III reviews *the indicators and evaluation frameworks* in use. The results of the survey and an analysis of 40 case studies are presented in Chapter IV *Synthesis of current experience*. Some central *issues and opportunities of integration* are taken up in Chapter V, before formulating *conclusions and recommendations* in Chapter VI. The report should provide useful guidelines for decision makers, road administrators, planners and designers on integrated processes. For researchers who are developing new planning approaches and tools, the report outlines some development needs in this area.

Field classification: Environment; Highway and transport planning; Accident studies.

Field number: 15, 21, 80.

Keywords: Accident prevention; corridor (transport); design; environment protection; evaluation; land use; landscaping; OECD; planning; regional planning; safety; urban area.

TABLE OF CONTENTS

EXECUTIVE SUMMARY

Within the OECD Road Transport Research Programme, a scientific expert Group was formed in 1995 to study how evaluation methods and planning tools can be designed and used to give equal and co-ordinated consideration to the safety and environmental effects of road transport. This report analyses the integration of these aspects into the agenda, design and implementation of transport policies. It focuses on complex transportation problems, at different territorial scales, especially in urban areas where the quality of the interaction between environmental and safety objectives is essential to a successful strategy.

The working method called for the group to:

- define the field of problems
- perform an international survey
- analyse the results of the survey
- make conclusions and proposals for developing an approach and evaluation serving an integrated process.

The response to the survey showed a great variation in the interpretation of and priority given to the theme of integrated strategies. Consequently the range of cases analysed in this report is limited, and the recommendations include aspects that could not be illustrated by the cases.

THE POTENTIAL FOR INTEGRATION

The current transport system is not on a sustainable path. Achievements in terms of mobility have at times come at a considerable environmental, social and economic cost. The challenge now is to find environmentally sound, socially equitable and economically viable ways of meeting transport needs. This places stringent demands on the transport system. The need for the integration of traffic safety and environmental concerns can be seen either as a need to co-ordinate these strategies with each other, or as the need to integrate both within an overall policy. In the long term, environmentally sustainable transport requires the integration of these concerns in the whole of transport policy.

Plans and projects generally take account of both traffic safety and environmental concerns, but each factor is normally dealt with individually. Possible explanations for this fragmented approach are the different focuses of the objectives, the involvement of different actors and an imbalance of know-how. Separate strategies may result in conflicting measures and administrative competition. Integrating environmental and safety strategy helps to identify conflicts at an early stage. If the process starts early enough, conflicts can often be avoided or resolved well before decisions are made. Integration also allows focusing resources in an efficient manner and gives a sound basis for setting priorities.

Many actors are involved in improving road safety and environmental protection. Their interests and objectives vary. The frameworks and their associated measures are constrained by economic and cultural considerations, but also by commitments made on a global level. The major problem of transport policy is to create a strategy for the development of different modes meeting a variety of objectives: economic efficiency, reliability and safety, and also environmental friendliness. The possibilities of integration depend on how policies are developed and how the relationships of policies applying to specific sectors are managed. Points of convergence and conflict can be identified by examining the elements in the transport system which are acted upon, and the instruments of the policies. Policies can be integrated if the measures employed to implement a policy support the objectives of other policies.

Considering the relation between traffic accidents and pollution, as exemplified by modelling, it is apparent that some variables are shared: traffic flow, speed and the composition and fluidity of traffic. On the individual level, there are common characteristics of vehicles, drivers, roads and traffic. The strategies which aim to prevent accidents and pollution and to reduce damage are based on the same principles of action: halting the increase in trips, improving the safety and environmental performance of vehicles, providing a safer road system that is compatible with sustainable development, promoting the use of modes which perform better with respect to safety and environmental protection and encouraging appropriate behaviour.

Vehicle design standards act at the source to reduce emissions and provide protection. Compliance with the standards does not usually result in conflicting measures. But there are cases where this needs special consideration. For instance, the improved occupant protection of a heavier car in relation to fuel use or impacts on other road users, or conversely, weight reduction to save energy as related to impact resistance. Improving vehicle use regulation, vehicle inspection and driver training supports both safety and environmental objectives.

Laws define general objectives and the basic means of action. At this level, sectoral policies, such as road policy, road safety policy and policies relating to other sectors, for instance regional planning, can be linked. Taxation, pricing of infrastructure and the service level offered influence users in their choice of transport mode. At the local level, many traffic management schemes have been introduced. If the objective is solely to reduce congestion, the effects on the environment and safety are not always positive. Limiting speeds, traffic and parking has positive consequences, but may increase risks outside the area concerned. Promotion of walking and cycling needs to be accompanied by safety measures.

There is a general tendency to revise the standards and the engineering of roads. This is probably the area in which there are the greatest number of possible conflicts and convergences between safety and environmental aspects. For example, there are conflicts involved in such measures as the use of noise barriers or de-icing salt and convergence in the uses of landscaping.

Urban structure is affected by several processes that increase travel demand. These are, to some extent, caused by the development of the transport system, especially the role of the passenger car. But travel and traffic conditions are not uniform, and the overall trends are only partially indicative of the actual changes in transport behaviour. Change is a characteristic of vital cities and towns, and no strategy can provide a permanently beautiful or healthy city, but there are means and measures to influence the processes of change. There is an extensive choice of measures to protect the environment or improve environmental quality. In addition to the transport system measures related above and local traffic management schemes, these concern land use planning and development control, the use of telematics, commuter policies, promoting public transport, setting up car-free zones and suiting goods transport logistics to urban conditions.

INDICATORS AND EVALUATION FRAMEWORKS

Indicators are needed to measure the incidence of problems as well as the impact on people's lives. When suitable indicators have been developed, the indicators related to the external effects (accident, pollution, noise, etc.) need to be combined so that the overall effect of a project or policy can be calculated to assist decision making. However, it is rare for decisions to be made in this way, and evaluation frameworks generally only guide or advise decision makers.

There is no universal set of indicators, but rather several sets to meet the needs of specific conceptual frameworks and purposes. The main indicators of particular relevance to safety and environmental aspects can be grouped as:

- Road and traffic indicators – overall traffic growth, modal split, capital expenditure for infrastructure, traffic management and flows, vehicle numbers.

- Safety indicators – number of people killed or injured, number of accidents, risks.

- Environmental impact indicators – Noise, vibration, air pollution, energy consumption, barrier effect and community severance, visual intrusion, cultural heritage and landscape values, water pollution, biological diversity, flora and fauna.

- Instruments indicators – taxation and subsidies, price structures.

- Process indicators – co-operation in institutions, management.

Many countries use systematic methods for evaluation and prioritisation of projects, but there is great variation in the methods: cost-benefit analysis, multi-criteria analysis, matrices, interaction diagrams and checklists. For major new projects, sophisticated integrated methods are often used, but for many other projects, environmental issues and road safety are often treated separately, if at all.

Cost-benefit analysis summarises all effects into a single value, which makes it easy to compare different options, but effects which cannot be valued in money terms are excluded and those that are valued may have a dubious value put on them. Multi-criteria analysis can deal with various units of measurement, but its methodology is not very transparent or easy to communicate.

CURRENT PRACTICES

Information on the definition of goals and the organisational responsibility for implementing them was collected in a survey of OECD Member countries.

The national level is generally the most important level in the definition of goals. Regional and local goals are often derived directly from the national goals. Goals on air quality are to a great extent influenced by international treaties, but there is a large diversity in the actual definition of the goals. Noise goals are expressed through accepted noise levels, but the consideration of exposure varies.

Almost all countries have goals for traffic safety, mainly expressed as reductions in the total number of fatalitiees and sometimes in the number of injured. The responsibilities for implementing the goals are usually spread among several ministries and central administrations as well as regional and local authorities.

The use of quantitative goals helps in putting a specific aspect into the evaluation and decision making process and leads to evaluation systems where the advantages and disadvantages of different alternatives are made explicit, but this does not automatically lead to choices favouring environmental or traffic safety aspects. Decisions are made at any given moment and in very different contexts. The essential need is to have explicit goals for both safety and environment and to be able to combine them in a way that is beneficial to both fields. When suitable goals are available, the weight given to them will depend on the decision context.

The cases received were extremely varied in nature, scope and geographical coverage. The group organised them according to two dimensions:

- Decision contexts: major infrastructure, corridor management, urban region transport planning, and norms, regulations and economic policies.

- Stages: policy and plan development, evaluation frameworks, implemented projects and policies.

Some 40 cases are presented. Though some countries' policy development cases show a strong trend towards integration, the number of cases exemplifying actual joint consideration of safety and environmental factors in implementation is not large. They mainly concern urban area traffic management and calming.

In addition to the case material, the group looked at the interaction between land use management and transport management in the context of urban policy. Existing recommendations for best practices build on the experiences of pilot cities seeking to improve the quality of life and service levels offered to their inhabitants, to restructure the traffic system as part of urban renewal and to manage traffic to increase the use of public transport, bicycling and walking. There is, as yet, limited experience in managing transport demand.

There were few cases exhibiting a conscious effort to treat safety and environmental objectives within an integrated framework. Most cases concern co-ordination of safety and environmental questions, whereas integration would imply an explicit trade-off between both. Considering weights and trade-offs in decision-making, fairness is difficult to achieve unless the impacts outside the immediate boundaries of the project scheme are taken into consideration.

The evaluation of multiple payoffs must involve looking beyond the immediate boundaries of the scheme or project. The evaluation methods which work best encourage decision makers to weigh this wider evidence. There is much room for innovation and experimentation, in interventions but particularly in evaluation frameworks and planning processes.

Some inferences can be drawn concerning the interventions which best serve safety and environmental goals, though there is not, at this time, a consensus on "best practice". Strategies for specific areas are both easier to assess and to implement than, for instance, general goals for travel demand reduction, and a growing number of administrations have undertaken ambitious urban redevelopment schemes.

From the experience of Member countries, it appears unreasonable to expect or seek the creation of new national institutions devoted solely to the integration or co-ordination of safety and environmental goals; the majority trend is towards decentralisation and deregulation. The lessons learnt from successful strategies suggest that it is feasible to make environmental and safety consequences more explicit in most technical and public assessments of proposed changes to transport and land use.

DEVELOPMENT TRENDS

The different approaches to traffic safety and environment are linked to the development of car use and traffic problems. The need for integration begins to be most strongly felt when both aspects are taken up as parts of a national transport policy, with a focus on reducing risk exposure and managing multiple transport modes. The role of the road environment in accidents is emphasised, as is the role of the road as a part of the whole environment. The change from looking at separate nuisances to a complex environment demands an increasing sophistication in the methods and frameworks used, as well as clear and operational targets.

Traffic safety and environmental objectives are given a position equal to service level objectives of the infrastructure. But giving the objectives equal weight does not assure equal implementation, and broad strategies may end up in a strictly nominal integration, behind which the decisions on major infrastructure projects remain uninfluenced. Thus, the wider the viewpoint adopted in a strategy, the greater is the need for specific, operational methods of assessing how schemes and projects implement strategic objectives. Public involvement increases the demand on the transparency of the assessment.

In the foreseeable future, it is unlikely that technological change will eliminate the problems of transportation and traffic, even if the potential for integration is fully exploited at the vehicle design and traffic management stages, taking into account the progress in new materials or sources of energy and telematics. Developing functional integrated strategies may be an inescapable requirement. Such travel demand factors as social, economic and cultural circumstances are only indirectly influenced by government or administrative action, but among those clearly influenced by public action, the transport system in its land use context does have a central role, as do governmental decisions on prices through taxation.

The development of road safety concerns has been described as "four paradigms in a century". Paralleling this, one can speak of the similar paradigms of environmental concerns, and foresee a fifth paradigm for an environmentally sustainable and intrinsically safe transport system. But this paradigm implies that the optimal result will not be found in the transport system alone. It demands the integration of aspects, institutions and activities of different administrative levels in different geographical areas.

There is a need to plan for a long time and with ambition. What is needed for succeeding is a management philosophy that will help to implement large scale changes in society. Such a management philosophy has to be generally independent of institutional and cultural differences between organisations, regions and countries. It can be realised with the aid of a hierarchical system of indicators, starting from a definition of the system, and then defining in two or three successive levels of indicators for planning and evaluation.

CONCLUSIONS

The environmental and traffic safety aspects of the transport system are closely related, but there are few cases showing a conscious effort to treat safety and environmental objectives within an integrated framework. More common is co-ordination through a simultaneous consideration of the two issues. There is a risk that action to improve one will be at the expense of the other. There are some clear advantages to the integration of road safety and environment protection: an increase in the benefits when an action contributes to both, or a better optimisation if an action contributes positively to one sector but negatively to the other. The problems of integration lie in the expansion of the sphere of action, the increasing number of criteria and of actors involved.

In an integrated strategy, a broad field of goals is systematically translated into a set of mutually reinforcing packages of measures. The focus is on improving the manner in which different actors recognise the need for co-operation and their readiness to implement it. The starting point is in improving communication and the dialogue between the different public administrations, the responsible authorities, the industry and the public.

The contents of a strategy are different at the national, regional and local levels, but the common need is a firm connection to land use planning. A long-term strategy presupposes a high level of integration. Its implementation in administrative action programmes is the stage where the cross-connections between different actions and the needs for co-operation can be clearly identified. Short-term action is divided according to the responsibilities of the actors involved and they should act in concert with one another, co-ordinating their measures as necessary.

In the form of alternative scenarios, visions of the future clarify the aims of the actors involved. The view of the present, and of what the problems are, should be shared by the actors. The problem formulation should be carefully considered, because it determines what kinds of measures are looked at.

A successful strategy needs firm objectives. Objectives that can be expressed as quantified targets have a prominent role, but not all concerns can be quantified. One way to address this is to set, instead, targets for the actions to improve performance. Another approach would be to ask the public to evaluate performance and needs. A strategy should also be flexible in regard to implementation, forming a process where the actors involved meet regularly to review how the objectives have been implemented and what changes are needed in future implementation.

Some key factors of the process contributing to the success of integration are an appropriate choice of public involvement, a detection of issues with special political or other connotations, an understanding of the paradoxes in what people will accept, a fair consideration for points of no return, a definition of possible packages of transport system measures, an identification of the gainers and losers from particular decisions and the possibility to learn from past failures as well as successes.

RECOMMENDATIONS

Transparency towards all actors involved is a prime concern. The consequences in regard to safety and environment should always be taken into account. In developing environmental policy, the safety aspects should be made explicit; in safety policy, the environmental aspects. A common set of indicators should be used. Developing environmental impact assessment to ensure that a sufficient range of environmental concerns are taken into account in implementation and further developing the use of the safety audit technique to serve early stages of planning may form an efficient way of bringing these concerns together.

The key indicators most reflective of the sustainability of the transport system are modal split, motor vehicle kilometrage and energy use   An overall increase in motor vehicle use or in vehicle kilometrage indicates a non-sustainable trend. However, such global indicators are insufficient to evaluate the efficiency of measures to reduce dependency on motor vehicles: more detailed indicators are needed which take into account the societal benefits and productivity of motorised travel, which are not constant on a vehicle-kilometre basis. Project objectives should also include the manner of dealing with such matters as severance and visual intrusion in urban areas, risks to the cultural heritage, fragmentation of natural areas, and water pollution.

To guide the setting of goals, an appropriately structured hierarchical system of indicators is needed. Technological, economical and regulative action should be considered as an entire package. To achieve more than a marginal impact on present trends, all of these have to be used. One should be aware that some groups of measures show clearly different relationships to the theme of integration.

Especially when large scale infrastructure schemes or wide-ranging regulatory or economic action are proposed, the risks of irreversible change should be carefully considered.

As a first step, each organisation responsible for a sector should undertake an impact evaluation study in the other sector. This implies a common set of indicators and an exchange of knowledge between the two sectors. At a later stage, the aim is designing an ecological and safe system of transport instead of corrective actions. It demands a higher level of integration between the parties and a new way to organise the process.

NEEDS FOR INNOVATION AND RESEARCH

There are still barriers between the safety and environment sectors which can only be reduced by a concerted research effort in the development of:

- Tools for testing and assessing policies,

- Pilot schemes to examine the implementation process and the technical effects of measures chosen,

- A common basis for vehicle and traffic flow data for models that predict accidents, pollutant emissions and noise,

- Models that both evaluate the impacts of changes in a road or area and forecast the long-term effects of changes in vehicle fleet composition or traffic flows,

- Data bases as well as models that take better account of all groups of pedestrians and bicyclists,

- More research into the environmental impacts of safety schemes, the safety impacts of environmental schemes and the social and societal impacts of such schemes.

Considering the planning and design process, further research is needed on process management, evaluation methodology and frameworks that allow multiple relevant dimensions or criteria to be taken into account in a transparent manner. Research is also needed on efficient ways to influence the public to promote safe and environmentally adapted travel changes. In regard to policies and measures, the main contemporary questions are:

- How to influence transport demand,
- How to increase the role of non-motorised traffic and, where appropriate, public transport in transport system implementation,
- Finding the packages of measures relevant for large urban areas,
- Responding to the process of rapid motorisation in developing economies.

OECD research is one channel for the exchange of know-how concerning the methods and measures which fit into a given situation. Further OECD studies could focus on specific applications of the approaches recommended in this report to one or more of these four underlying issues.

The work of this Group has revealed a modest, but growing, awareness of the need to make the safety and environmental balance-sheets coherent and accessible, as a normal part of road transport planning. In some cases, even posing the question served to raise that awareness.

CHAPTER I INTRODUCTION

Separate strategies acting toward shared safety and environmental aims can potentially result in overall improvement even if they are not specifically co-ordinated. But separate strategies may also have unfortunate results. For example, conflicts may arise regarding roadside trees in that they are an essential factor in the landscape, but may pose a serious traffic safety risk. The strategies for safety and the strategies for environment may therefore result in conflicting measures and administrative competition.

> "It is rarely possible to force reluctant agencies or governmental bodies to do things that they do not want or support. It is therefore to be expected that some programmes will be only partly implemented. This point underscores the importance of ensuring maximum consensus before a programme is formally adopted, in order to enhance the likelihood of implementation" (1).

Integrating safety and environment strategies will help to identify possible conflicts at an early stage. If the process starts early enough, conflicts can be avoided or resolved well before decisions are made. Integration also makes it possible to focus resources in an efficient manner. Integration offers a sound basis for setting priorities, as these are developed within and during the process of creating the strategy.

Recognising the value of improved strategies as well as the need for a substantive international review of current practices, the OECD Road Transport Research Programme established in 1995 a Scientific Expert Group to perform an international study of comprehensive evaluation methods and planning tools for the safety and environmental effects of road traffic in urban areas. The study was extended to include the planning and improvement of roads outside built-up areas. This is an interdisciplinary task that required specialists and researchers from many fields. The group was constituted with special regard to traffic safety, environmental, urban design, and economic expertise.

This report analyses the questions of integrating traffic safety and environmental aspects into transport policies, planning and design, and discusses possible solutions to the problems arising. The purpose is to develop ideas and methods that can be used for planning co-ordinated strategies. The abstract nature of the task required the Group to look at the planning process as well as its practical contents.

I.1. THE CASE FOR INTEGRATION

The need for integration can be seen either as a need to integrate environment and safety strategies with each other, or as the need to integrate both within an overall transport policy. In the long term, environmentally sustainable transport requires a level of integration corresponding to the latter:

> "A wide range of policy instruments exists to redirect urban travel through land use planning and transport policy..., but no single one of them has the power to achieve the objectives of sustainable development: to do this, governments need to introduce packages of mutually reinforcing policies" (2).

For the short term, the prime need is to ensure the productive interaction of environmental and safety strategies while seeking a balance within the larger scope of transport policy. Some examples of this are:

- The formulation of quantitative goals as a basis for policy integration.

- Respecting the wider context of impacts; it is important to define the geographical sphere of influence for all essential factors in order to be able to bring the decision on the whole of a project to the appropriate administrative level.

- The transport corridor approach. Typical examples are accident reduction measures and environmental adaptation of urban through roads. Dealing with a given road and its surroundings, its users and neighbours alike, facilitates seeking a holistic solution.

- A comprehensive approach for urban areas. This approach recognises the need to ensure acceptable mobility, while taking environment and safety into account. An example of this is traffic reduction and calming strategies that can produce marked improvements of both safety and environmental quality in the areas concerned.

- Using overall regulatory instruments, taxation or market incentives, to achieve complex objectives, for instance toll rings to regulate inner city traffic flows, simultaneously directing long distance traffic to better adapted and safer routes outside inner city areas.

One central issue is to find a strategy that considers the relationships between safety and environment as well as objectives of urban development. The strategy needs to be adapted to different circumstances and stages of development. Because it has to provide a structure for setting priorities in a very wide range of conflicts, it must be comprehensive. The strategic choices concern a wide range of actors, from the general public to the decision-makers in the different sectors. A specific problem is raised by the semi-urban and fringe areas surrounding large city centres. In these, major changes in land use and infrastructure often take place without sufficient regard to their interaction with the existing structure.

On the methodological level, there is a need for prediction methods that take a multiplicity of factors into account in a transparent manner. Such methods could be used to evaluate the effects of a proposed new transport plan alternative and the effects of a specific new road stretch or traffic calming project, as well as to identify exposure or risk on the present network.

I.2. THE SCOPE OF THE REPORT

This report focuses on complex situations where the quality of the interaction between environmental and safety objectives is essential to a successful strategy. This is typical for urban areas where the greatest concentration of problems is encountered. However, the discussion is also relevant to semi-urban and rural areas where complicated terrain, sensitive natural features or substantial loads on the environment limit the possibilities of resolving transport problems. The OECD Conference on "Towards Sustainable Transportation", held in March 1996 in Vancouver, noted that:

> "Most movement of people and much movement of freight occur in urban areas. Urban areas are the focus of even more concern about transportation than might be expected from the amounts of movement there, because of the concentration of vehicles and the proximity of people to them. Local pollution from transport activity is overwhelmingly a phenomenon of urban areas, but the global impacts of transportation are less so" (3).

The report aims to provide recommendations for decision makers, road administrators, planners and designers. For researchers who are developing new planning approaches and tools, the report seeks to outline some development needs in this area.

The report recognises that strategic decision-making involves the political process of communities and society as a whole. This must be taken into account in any application of the proposals and recommendations of this report, to avoid the risk of creating a process closed to the public. The different viewpoints of actors inside and outside the transport sector can meet only if the strategy process is transparent to public evaluation and debate.

I.3. THE GROUP'S APPROACH

The subject is approached using two perspectives:

- Looking at the institutions that are responsible for traffic safety and the environment, and at those that have the task of implementing road and transport planning, vehicle inspection, driver education, and traffic monitoring, and

- Looking at methods that make it possible to carry out comprehensive evaluations of the environmental and traffic safety impacts of road transport.

National strategies to address traffic safety and environmental problems are surveyed. National, regional and local institutional frameworks are analysed to show how the political strategies and goals are implemented in the different institutions. An integrated and comprehensive view of the safety and environmental aspects of transport demands looking at the transport system and land use as a whole, with all the actors involved. A central factor in such a holistic approach is the people living in and using the area in question.

The present methods that have the potential to comprehensively evaluate the impacts of transport are examined. Such evaluation methods have been developed using the results of studies on topics such as:

- health risks,
- the nuisance people feel in relation to different environmental and safety factors,
- accident or environmental costs avoided,
- the willingness to pay for, or other valuation of reducing nuisances or risks,
- hedonic pricing, such as relating real estate prices to nuisance or disturbance levels.

One issue is whether the evaluation methods can be integrated within a cost-benefit assessment structure or within a non-monetary multicriteria framework. These methods are used in many countries for seeking optimal alternatives, but the optimisation principles upon which they are based meet with criticism as being inappropriate to the process of decision-making.

> "Formal techniques, including cost-benefit, multi-attribute utility and cost-effectiveness analyses, can assist in making trade-offs between conflicting targets. But in the end, the output of any formal analysis must obtain political support, if it is to be implemented" (1).

There is also a need to take account of the long term development in transport and communication technology and the impacts it can have on any choice of strategy.

The working method of the group was:

- define the field of problems,
- perform an international survey using a questionnaire and referring to case studies,
- analyse the results of the survey,
- make conclusions and propose guiding principles for an integrated process.

Based on the outline of the problem presented in this chapter, Chapter II sets out the context of integrated strategies and Chapter III reviews the indicators and evaluation frameworks currently being used. The results of the survey are presented in Chapter IV. Some central issues of integration are taken up in Chapter V in order to introduce the conclusions and recommendations of the Group in Chapter VI.

The response to the survey showed a great variation in the interpretation of and priority given to the theme of integrated strategies. Consequently the range of cases analysed in this report is limited, and the recommendations include aspects that could not be illustrated by the cases.

Table I.1. lists the countries that replied to the survey. The replies differed largely from one country to another. Some countries provided the Group with comprehensive information, including detailed case studies, while others only gave general comments.

I.4. PARALLEL, BUT SEPARATE STRATEGIES

The current transport system is not on a sustainable path. The admirable achievements in terms of mobility have come at some considerable environmental as well as social and economical costs. The challenge now is to find ways of meeting transportation needs that are environmentally sound, socially equitable and economically viable. While each of these are important aspects of sustainability, their difference need to be recognised, and subsequently reconciled when developing sustainable transport polices and strategies. Sustainable development places stringent demands on the transport system. In accordance with a qualitative definition proposed in an OECD study on environmental criteria for sustainable transport, the system should provide

"transport that does not endanger public health or ecosystems and meets mobility needs consistent with:

a)   use of renewable resources at below their rates of regeneration,

b)   use of non-renewable resources at below the rates of development of renewable substitutes" (4).

The OECD study recognised that this is a long-term concept, to be achieved through the attainment of several intermediate steps. In many countries, such intermediate steps have been formulated as specific goals and objectives for the transport sector as well as for other sectors of the economy. In this framework, goals are set for the reduction of energy consumption, CO_2 emissions, air pollution, noise, and other important factors.

Sustainable transport systems will not be achieved in the short-term and, due to varying economic, environmental and social conditions between and within countries, there is no single best way to realise them. As was concluded by a series of international Round Tables on reconciling safety, the environment and mobility needs :

"The consequent challenge is to enable people in countries of different kinds to benefit from road traffic in ways which are acceptable in the short term and sustainable in the long term" (5).

There is however a set of guiding principles upon which transition strategies should be built. These principles stress the importance of:

- providing access for people to goods and services rather than mobility;
- ensuring social, inter-regional and inter-generational equity;
- enhancing individual and community responsibility;
- protecting health and safety and enhancing the quality of life;
- promoting education, public participation and information support;
- fostering integrated planning approaches;
- encouraging sustainable use of land and other natural resources;
- preventing pollution;
- ensuring economic well-being.

Improving road traffic safety has long been an essential goal for road authorities. Every motorised country has a road safety programme in that the responsible authorities carry out a set of organised activities intended to improve road safety (1). However, as environmental and other priorities have been brought forward, traffic safety has often been taken for granted.

The trend to integrate the principles of sustainable development into land use planning has also set new challenges for road and transport planning. National goals are agreed upon at the political level and implemented through different institutions. As well, many local authorities work to integrate road safety and environmental aspects in town and traffic planning. The multiplicity of actors creates its own set of challenges that must be addressed if sustainable principles are to be successfully implemented.

The impacts of a transport system on health, environment and welfare, which have to be considered in such a planning process, are extremely diverse. In addition, perceptions of the relative importance of environmental quality, road safety and fluid traffic vary according to the predominance of road traffic in a country's transport system and especially according to the level of dependence on private motor vehicles. Plans, such as national transport plans, regional or city transport plans, or new road designs, generally take account of both traffic safety and environmental concerns, but each factor is normally dealt with individually. Where they exist, there are separate:

- prediction models,
- guidelines and norms,
- planning objectives,
- strategies, and
- risk management systems for each effect.

There are several possible explanations for this fragmented approach. One consideration is the different focus of safety and environmental objectives. Another consideration is that there are different actors involved. Responsibility for implementing road safety measures is divided between different levels of government, different policy-making bodies and executive agencies, with other bodies and agencies responsible for implementing environmental measures. There is also at present an imbalance of know-how. Road administrations have dealt with safety concerns for decades, while serious study of environmental aspects is fairly recent. Additional skills and the involvement of professions other than those traditionally involved in road management are needed. The following chapters provide an in-depth analysis of these concerns and provide possible approaches that can lead to better integration of safety and environment strategies.

I.5. REFERENCES

1. OECD. ROAD TRANSPORT RESEARCH (1994). *Targeted Road Safety Programmes*. OECD, Paris.

2. OECD/ECMT (1995). *Urban Travel and Sustainable Development*. OECD, Paris.

3. OECD. Environment Directorate (1997). *Towards Sustainable Transportation*, Proceedings of the International Conference, organised by the OECD and hosted by the Government of Canada, Vancouver, British Columbia, 24-27 March 1996, OECD, Paris.

4.   OECD. Environment Directorate (1996). *Environmental Criteria for Sustainable Transport.* Report on Phase 1 of the Project on Environmentally Sustainable Transport. OCDE/GD(96)136, Paris.

5.   ALLSOP, R.E. (1993). *Agenda for Safe Access in a Stable Environment: Issues for decision-makers as identified at the International Scientific Initiatives on Road Traffic Round Tables, 1989-1991.* International Association of Traffic and Safety Science (IATSS), Tokyo.

6.   OECD. ROAD TRANSPORT RESEARCH (1994). *Environmental Impact Assessment of Roads.* OECD, Paris.

7.   OECD. ROAD TRANSPORT RESEARCH (1997). *Outlook 2000.* Report of the 30th Anniversary. OECD, Paris.

CHAPTER II   THE POTENTIAL FOR INTEGRATION

II.1. A LARGE NUMBER OF ACTORS, WITH DIFFERING APPROACHES

A large number of actors are involved in improving road safety and environmental protection: the public sector (the central government with its agencies, local and regional authorities, public transport companies, regulated concessions), the private sector (the vehicle manufacturing and oil industries, civil engineering companies), citizens' and environmental groups, other associations, international institutions, etc. The amount of interest which these actors accord to safety and environmental matters depends greatly on their strategy, which is revealed by the relative importance given to these objectives and the development of mobility (1).

Vehicle manufacturers, for example, have always been interested in passive safety as a means of providing occupant crash protection. It is only recently that they have begun to consider environmental protection, for example by developing low fuel use and low emission vehicles. The designers of roads and interurban motorways may consider environmental protection a cause of gridlock or delays and find the integration of safety difficult because of the imperatives of traffic flow and capacity. In urban areas, town planners and engineers are now giving greater importance to environmental and safety objectives. However, the dominance of the motor car still governs attitudes, although it is beginning to lose ground in many countries. Elected representatives of local government have generally given priority to reducing congestion, either as a means of reducing the journey times for motorists or in order to assist the operation of public transport. As a result, environmental and safety objectives may take second place.

Public policies with respect to transport and environmental protection are often aimed at specific sectors and are sometimes contradictory. The trade-off between economic development and quality of life is a social issue which must be faced by every country and one which makes it necessary to question some systems of values. There is also a trade-off between the actions of citizens' and environmental groups and the official decision-making process. This trade-off develops new attitudes to environmental policies and safety.

II.2. FROM LOCAL SENSITIVITY TO GLOBAL AWARENESS

Transport impacts on the environment at all levels, both world-wide through the greenhouse effect and locally with, for instance, air and noise pollution, and in both the short and long terms. The health effects of air pollution are less apparent and often more long term and cumulative in nature but affect a large number of persons, whereas the injuries suffered by road users in accidents are more violent and immediate, but are limited to a smaller number of persons.

As a result of the differences in the nature and scale of the risks, the frameworks of measures (decision-making and implementation), in the combat against accidents and pollution, will be more or less constrained by economic considerations, cultural factors, but also by commitments made on a global level. The sensitivity of the public to air pollution has increased. The risk is of a passive nature and as yet ill-defined. The risk of accidents is active in nature, and the public is less motivated, in spite of the ultimately far greater consequences for the individual.

In connection with environmental pollution, political leaders are subjected to pressure from the public which is concerned by local pollution problems, but also from the need to comply with international agreements made at conferences such as those at Stockholm, Rio de Janeiro, Montreal and Berlin. International political influence seems much less evident in the area of road safety. In this area there is still the danger of a degree of isolation as regards the attitudes towards safety or the environment. However, organisations such as the European Union and the OECD are placing increasing importance on the concept of sustainable mobility or transport (2) which attempts to integrate environmental and safety objectives.

II.3. AN INCREASE IN THE COMPLEXITY OF ENVIRONMENTAL CONCERNS

After the period of the major national regulatory road safety measures concerning speed limits, the wearing of seat belts and drunk driving, risk reduction strategies have moved towards the launching of local policies which give more responsibility and resources to local and regional governments and towards the integration of road safety measures within a programme which co-ordinates the efforts of different actors to combat accidents on the basis of a more comprehensive diagnosis of safety (3) which is specifically adapted to urban areas (4). Multi-disciplinary and systematic analysis of accidents has removed the barriers between different sectors of primary safety (before the crash), secondary safety (crash phase) and tertiary safety (aftermath) or those directed at one of three components, the vehicle, the road, and the driver (3).

Environmental concerns, which were later to appear, are constantly developing and increasing in complexity. The initial stage, which was essentially centred on the protection of nature on a small scale, kept safety and environmental objectives in isolation from one another for a considerable time. The effects of air pollution on the health of city dwellers require not just an environmental perspective but a public health perspective, in the same way that the problem of accidents was taken much more seriously once it was viewed not simply as a transport problem but also as a public health problem. A parallel can be drawn between the two on the basis of an analysis of the risks which road traffic causes to users and residents, with a view to achieving integrated, or even common, risk management. While the risks have a common origin, namely road traffic, the risks are better identified for road traffic accidents than for air pollution as a result of the diversity of the sources of pollutant emissions and their simultaneous presence in the air which makes risk assessment difficult.

There has also been a shift in environmental interest toward urban areas and sustainable development. This shift has helped break down the separation between safety and environmental objectives, particularly in the context of urban policies.

II.4. THE INTERACTIONS BETWEEN PUBLIC POLICIES

The problems shared by road safety and environmental protection are tackled by governments using public policies which influence the behaviour of consumers and companies (see Table II.1). However, it is not unusual for public policies to interact or interfere with each other. Fuel taxation has social, economic, environmental and political repercussions which go beyond the transport sector. Some policies at one time limit the effectiveness of others, and at other times increase it. A specific policy may include measures which, while complying with the objectives which have been set, run counter to other objectives which are also desirable. When conflict occurs, priority is often given to short term objectives over long term ones. This is one of the reasons why it is difficult to integrate public health and environmental protection considerations within public policies.

This rule also applies to the transport sector. The major challenge for transport policy is to create an intersectorial strategy for the development of different modes (road, rail, air, navigable waterways) which must meet a variety of objectives – economic efficiency, reliability, mobility, safety and environmental friendliness. In general, it is very difficult to resolve all conflicts, particularly those between mobility and safety (5), mobility and the environment, and safety and the environment. It is the role of public policy to make decisions on the basis of costs and benefits in order to resolve the problem when all of the dimensions of conflict have already been identified.

The possibility of integrating the concerns of environmental protection and road safety depends on the different levels at which these public policies are developed and implemented. Consider the possibility of "vertical integration" between four levels of government:

- supranationally or federally,
- nationally: Governments,
- regionally: provinces, counties,
- locally: towns and cities.

An inter-sectoral approach is superimposed on this trans-territorial approach and attempts to use "horizontal integration" in order to manage the relationships among the policies which apply to specific sectors by harmonising objectives, integrating the action programmes which make use of a range of instruments, co-ordinating those responsible for implementing policies and standardising assessment methods.

The main instruments which have direct consequences on both the environment and road safety can be based on (6):

- Regulations which lay down technical standards or impose restrictions on access to driving or to the network with accompanying penalties.

- Investment in transport infrastructure and public transport services.

- Economic incentives, either "negative" (taxation) or positive (subsidies).

- Social communication and administrative management in order to inform the public more fully concerning the nature of policies as a means of gaining greater support, contacts with companies in order to make voluntary agreements, and intersectorial and geographical co-ordination between different authorities.

Table II.1. **Typical objectives, instruments of implementation and actors with respect to public policies**

Public policy	Objective	Level of decision-making	Instruments	Main actors
Motor vehicle	• Improving the performance of new vehicles: noise, pollution, fuel consumption, safety • Maintenance of vehicles already on the road	• Supranational or national • National	• Manufacturing standards, R&D finance for new technologies • Vehicle checks	• Government Departments, motor vehicle manufacturers, oil industry • Inspection agencies
Transport system	• Improving the efficiency of the transport system (modal choice)	• Supranational • National • Regional • Local	• Planning, internalising costs • Pricing, scheduling of investments, regulations • Planning, scheduling of investments • Regulation, investment, urban travel plans	• Government, Ministries • Government, Ministries • Regional and local Authorities, Network operators • Local authorities, network operators
Roads	• Improving the design and operation of road network	• National /Regional • Local	• Standards (geometric design) speed limits, telematics, tolling • By-passes, traffic management, improvements (traffic calming, 30 km/h zones), urban tolls	• Ministry • Local authorities
Air pollution	• Limiting emissions	• Supranational/ National	• Exposure standards	• Ministries
Noise pollution	• Limiting the exposure of residents to noise	• National/ Regional/ Local	• Exposure standards, Remedial programme	• Ministries, Local and regional Authorities
Road safety	• Reducing casualties	• National • Regional • Local	• Regulations, investments, incentives, communication management	• Government Ministries and organisations • Local authorities
Land use	• Sustaining economic and social development	• National/ Regional/local	• Investments, regulations	• Ministries • Local authorities
Water pollution	• Controlling quality	• National/local	• Regulations, remedial programmes	• Ministries, Regional authorities
Biodiversity	• Preserving species	• National	• Regulations	• Ministries

Table II.2 shows how these instruments are applied. The applicability may differ from the presentation of this table depending on the specific formulation of the measure concerned.

Different levels of government use these instruments to varying degrees. Regulation by means of standards is used at the supranational level, both in order to attack global environmental problems (greenhouse effect) and in order to ensure that national industries remain competitive. Pricing policy (levies and taxes) belongs more to the national domain as do major investments. At the local level, the authorities tackle road traffic accidents, and noise and air pollution by regulations and investment instruments. They may also use planning as an active and sometimes comprehensive instrument.

Table II.2. **Instruments available for achieving road safety and selected environmental protection objectives** (X= Major impact)

Instruments	Impacts			
	Accident	Noise	Air pollution	Energy/CO_2
1. Regulations				
Vehicle standards				
• active/passive safety	X			
• size/weight/power	X			X
• emission (pollutants, noise)		X	X	
• energy efficiency				X
Town and country planning standards				
• density, zoning		X	X	
• construction		X		
Infrastructure standards				
• safety improvements	X			
• noise		X		
Vehicle checks	X		X	X
Speed limits (type of road/zone)	X	X	X	
Protective equipment	X			
Control of drunk driving	X			
Working conditions of truck drivers	X			
Drivers' licensing	X			
Certification of transport undertaking	X			
Restrictions	X	X	X	
Penalties for traffic offences	X			
2. Public investments				
Roads, streets (design, surface, roadside)	X	X		
Cycle tracks	X			
Roundabouts, squares	X			
By-passes	X	X	X	
Intermodal co-ordination				
• park&ride facilities		X	X	X
• combined freight transport	X	X	X	X
Traffic management systems	X		X	
Public transport			X	X
Emergency services	X			
3. Economic incentives				
Insurance premiums	X			
Fines	X			
Vehicle purchase, annual road taxes		X	X	
Fuel taxes				X
Road tolls		X	X	X
Urban tolls		X	X	X
Parking charges		X	X	
Public transport subsidies			X	X
4. Communication management				
Education in schools	X			
Driver training	X	X	X	
Information campaigns	X		X	
Voluntary standards	X		X	X
Consultation			X	
Co-ordination between sectors	X	X	X	X

The principal categories of instruments consist of a variety of measures which are directed at vehicles, road users, traffic, infrastructure and town planning, and may concern either road safety or environmental protection. These measures are applied differently in the context of each of three main dimensions:

- The segment of traffic: travellers (work/study, leisure, shopping), goods (long distance/distribution),
- The type of vehicle and fuel,
- The interurban and urban (inner city, outer city) network.

Regulatory measures are coercive in nature and demand the introduction of a system of monitoring and enforcement. The running costs of a regulatory-based system will be greater when a large number of persons who are highly dispersed are affected, such as in the case of motorists. Economic measures are directed at the users and aim to achieve a change in behaviour. Money and the marketplace are used as a universal mediator to harmonise individual interests, but care should be taken to ensure that economic measures do not completely take the place of policy. The benefit of a market approach stems from income recycled from these measures that can be used by the government or local and regional authorities to finance actions which support a policy or which reduce the burden of taxation on other sectors (employment).

The provision of transport infrastructure is the most tangible example of the commitment of government, although there is perhaps a tendency to seek infrastructure investment rather than to optimise the system. Social communication and administrative management instruments are used to manage the relationship between the public authorities and private companies and citizens. They are based on information, education, consultation and negotiation. One implication of the management aspect is also that the position of experts and the scientific community in the progress of the debate prior to the taking of a decision is not as clear as was previously the case.

II.5. POINTS OF CONVERGENCE AND CONFLICT

Possible points of convergence and conflict between the objectives of environmental protection and road safety can be identified qualitatively by examining the parameters of the elements in the road transport system which are acted upon in order to achieve these objectives and by examining the policy instruments that are intended to modify these variables. The possibility for convergence or conflict between the objectives will be determined by the extent to which the different policies share the same instruments and measures.

Conceptually, it is possible to integrate policies if the measures employed in order to implement one policy conform with the objectives of the other policies. Co-ordinating the measures associated with different sectors and geographical zones within a common strategy, that guarantees coherence, and therefore convergence, is based on a theory of underlying change. The theory should be commonly understood and capable of foreseeing the road safety and environmental impacts of the measures and their combinations. To an even greater extent, convergence will rely on all actors sharing a political desire for integration.

For example, in the light of the fact that the distribution of speed is a factor which is associated with both accident risk and air pollution, it is possible to reduce simultaneously the number of road fatalities and the amounts of pollutants which are emitted on interurban and urban road networks. However, political decisions can contradict this, as in the USA where speed limit regulations of 55 mph on the Interstate network were liberated by a decision which was taken in order to favour mobility (5), when the 55 mph speed limit had been introduced in 1973 in order to save energy and reduce the number of road fatalities.

This analysis is a summary because objectives are considered in a general way without an attempt to examine details. Local conflicts which can be unequal in nature whereby the benefits are obtained by one part of society at a high cost to another, are more difficult to consider because they are more dependent on the specific conditions which relate to the measures. An assessment of a by-pass around a built-up zone in terms of accidents and air and noise pollution will be more or less favourable depending on the geographic zones into which the area is broken down. What one district in a town or city gains as a result of traffic restraint measures can be lost in neighbouring districts as a result of transferred traffic, if the necessary accompanying measures have not been taken for political, technical or economic reasons. It is thus necessary to study the policies which are implemented in the field in order to reveal the decision processes which have taken place.

II.5.1. A set of risk factors

As soon as any attempt is made to act or intervene, a theory of change (7) applies. Such a theory is a representation of the mechanisms of action by which the introduced measures will change the state of the system. This representation is based on a scientific understanding of the factors that lead to accidents and various forms of pollution. Road transport research on accidents and pollution has produced models of varying degrees of sophistication which identify the key factors that affect the frequency and severity of road accidents, the amount of air pollutants emitted or the noise levels reached and the associated health consequences of each.

At the network or partial network (road section, intersection, district) levels, the rate of injury and damage accidents, the rates of emissions per vehicle or per person kilometre and the noise levels will depend on traffic flow which is characterised by the average and the variance of the speed of flow. Traffic flow is conditioned by the composition of traffic and the degree of traffic congestion (free flow/congested).

Accidents, air pollution and noise levels increase with traffic level variables such as flow, average speed and dispersion of speed, though the relationship between speed and some air pollutant emissions is complex. These relationships will depend on traffic conditions determined by vehicle mix (pedestrians, bicycles, two-wheeled motorised vehicles, passenger cars, light commercial vehicles, lorries, buses and others) and the degree of congestion.

While an increase in flow, average speed or the dispersion of speeds leads to more accidents, emissions of pollutants and noise, the effect of traffic composition and congestion is to modify this trend. For a particular volume of traffic, the functions of the indicators will vary according to composition of traffic. Differences among road users as regards their vulnerability to collisions (pedestrians and light two-wheeled vehicles as opposed to passenger cars and lorries) lead to completely different accident and casualty statistics, and the same applies to emissions and noise levels. Freely flowing and congested traffic does not produce the same accident frequencies (accidents are more frequent but less severe in dense traffic) nor the same levels of pollutant emissions (in dense traffic, these are higher as a result of the increased number of stops and starts). It is important to make a distinction between different types of pollutants: HC, CO_2, NOX, VOC, particulates from fuel combustion or road dust as their relative quantities can vary.

At the individual vehicle or the driver, the risk of being involved in an accident, the rate of emissions per kilometre driven or the level of engine or tyre/road contact noise is related to the characteristics of:

- the vehicle (weight, loading, age),
- the engine (type of fuel, power) and the tyres,
- the driver (age, sex, state, style of driving),
- the road (surface, profile, etc.),
- the way the vehicle is used (speed, acceleration/deceleration),
- the weather.

The mechanical energy dissipated during accidents, the pollutants and noise will all damage health through specific mechanisms which must be modelled. The physical damage and injuries which occur during an accident are due to the exposure of users (occupants, vehicles, pedestrians, cyclists) to the mechanical energy which is dissipated in the collision during a very short period of time. It follows that the severity of the injuries will be caused by the characteristics of:

- the vehicle (weight, structure),
- the users (age, protection),
- the collision (difference of speed or reduction in speed at the instant of impact, angle of impact),
- the accident scenario (collision with an obstacle, between two vehicles, overturning).

In the case of air pollution, the harm to human beings is caused by the toxicity of the pollutants. For the longer term, the harmful effects of pollutants depend on the ambient concentration of the pollutant in the air and the exposure which is measured by the amount of time spent in polluted environments. Dose/effect relationships obtained from toxicological and epidemiological studies are used to set limits for tolerable concentrations per unit of time. The dose/effect relationship differs from one individual to another depending on their vulnerability. Vulnerability tends to be higher for elderly persons, very young children and those who are already in poor health with conditions such as asthma. The ambient concentration is the result of physical processes, chemical reactions and dispersion phenomena which are difficult to model, in particular as pollutants may react with each other. Exposure to an individual pollutant is often difficult to assess as pollutants frequently form mixtures.

Scientific understanding of accidents and pollution assists in identifying the most effective forms of action by making it possible to select the factors which have the greatest effect on the frequency and severity of accident and pollution phenomena. The models can in turn be used in order to quantify the impacts of the measures which are considered in a policy by the use of scenarios of change and in order to judge how suitable and coherent the measures are as a means of achieving the set aims. The Swedish EVA model is a good example (8). In particular, it provides a means of assessing the environmental impacts (noise and air pollution) and the safety impacts of road investments both at the project and national planning levels.

It is apparent from the overview of models that some dependent variables are common to the areas of accident risk and emissions of pollutants and noise. These are, at a macroscopic level, traffic flow, speed (average speed and dispersion), the composition and fluidity of traffic, all of which must be controlled in order to reduce the frequency of accidents and the level of emissions. At the individual level the characteristics of the following can be added:

- the vehicles: weight, power, age,
- the drivers: age, state, style of driving,
- the roads: surface, profile,
- the traffic: free flow/stop-start/congested.

The effects of these should be examined in greater detail in order to identify the convergences.

In terms of severity, all those exposed to risk do not have the same level of vulnerability. Pedestrians and some groups such as young children and the elderly are particularly vulnerable to all types of risk. However, these groups share few variables as the mechanisms involved are different.

II.5.2. *Means of action*

Strategies aimed at preventing accidents and pollution as well as reducing the damage caused by them are based on the same principles of action:

- halting the increase in trip-making,
- improving the safety and environmental performance of vehicles,
- providing a road system which is safe and compatible with sustainable development,
- promoting the use of modes which perform better with respect to safety and environmental protection,
- encouraging behaviour which is safe and which respects the environment.

Road vehicles

Design

Vehicle design standards act at the source to reduce vehicle emissions, to fix the maximum speed, to provide occupant crash protection and to make vehicles less aggressive in the event of impact with other road users.

Vehicle noise emissions, pollutant emissions and impact resistance are the subject of regulations (USA, EU) which in particular take the form of standards which are applied in the course of vehicle approval and which are becoming gradually more severe over time by taking advantage of technological progress.

Other parameters that are currently the subject of regulations and constitute points of convergence or conflict between the environment and road safety include maximum speed and; the weight, size and power of vehicles, in particular lorries and motorcycles (at the project stage). Appraisal is difficult in the case of this conflict as an increase in the size of lorries increases their capacity and reduces the number of trips (therefore the amount of emissions) but increases their aggressiveness in crashes, of which, however, there should be fewer. However, the limitations of lorry speeds which are imposed during the manufacturing process assist both the objectives of safety and emission reduction.

It should also be noted that what is gained in energy efficiency is used as a resource by motor vehicle manufacturers in order to increase the weight and power of those vehicles which are not regulated. This has an uncertain impact on safety. A heavy car provides better occupant protection, but causes greater injuries to the occupants of small vehicles. The additional power is used to increase driving speeds and will result in more accidents. Attention must be given to the compatibility between weights and the structures of road transport modes. Standards for the structure of the front ends of vehicles are currently being prepared in order to reduce the severity of the injuries to pedestrians and cyclists in the event of an impact. Reducing risk encourages the use of modes of transport which are vulnerable in traffic and the resulting modal transfer contributes to environmental protection.

Finally, change and the development of new technologies such as electric vehicles can lead to situations of conflict or convergence depending on the extent to which the design of the vehicle integrates safety. For example, the silent propulsion of electric vehicles means that they must be fitted with devices which make them noticeable to pedestrians. The conflict involved in reducing the weight of vehicles with a view to energy savings, while retaining sufficient impact resistance, will require the use of new materials. The use of new methods of propulsion can also reduce the danger of fuel igniting in a crash.

Use

The right to operate a vehicle – passenger car, lorry, motorised two-wheeled vehicle – is regulated by the need to have a licence. By fixing the conditions for obtaining such a licence (age, physical ability), it is possible to exclude that part of the population which is at the two extremes – the young and the old – from access to motorised modes. These groups are channelled towards public transport, walking or bicycles, which are economical in terms of energy but have higher accident exposure in the absence of specific measures.

More severe conditions regulate access to the transport profession. Freight transport undertakings are encouraged by training and certification to conduct safety and environmental audits within their organisations.

Vehicle purchase, registration and annual road taxes are all factors that can influence motorists to choose vehicles which pollute less. The cost of fuel influences the distances covered by passenger cars and lorries. The inclusion of an environmental tax would limit the use of these two modes of transport, which would result in a reduction in emissions and accidents. Government premiums which are paid when a vehicle is purchased encourage households to replace their car, speeding up renewal of the vehicle fleet which thereby becomes more efficient and safer. There is, however, the counterproductive result of an increase in the distances covered by new vehicles. The old vehicles driven by either young persons, the elderly or members of the workforce with low incomes, do not result in higher risk as it is in the interest of these drivers to preserve their vehicle and compensate risk by driving more carefully. A replacement will not be paid for by their insurance. On the other hand, the level of emissions is considerably higher.

Insurance premiums send an economic signal to vehicle owners as the sum payable depends on the power of the vehicle. The system of no-claims bonuses and surcharges reinforces dissuasion but means that drivers fail to make a proportion of possible claims in order to avoid a price increase. It should be noted that not all accidents costs are internalised in the insurance charge. The penalty points licence system provides a means of modifying the behaviour of a multi-offending minority of drivers and encouraging the majority of drivers to comply better with the Highway Code, but requires a costly administrative and legal organisation. Economic measures which affect the individual rather than a group of individuals are more efficient.

In addition, maintenance operations and vehicle checks provide a typical example of a point of convergence. With reference to road safety, the braking and lighting system and the condition of tyres are checked; with reference to the environment, CO and CO_2 emissions and the condition of the silencer on the exhaust (but not as yet noise emissions) are checked.

Driver training

A distinction should be made between young drivers learning how to drive and the training of professional drivers. Evidence is varied on the accident reduction, energy conservation and air quality benefits of driver training. Driver training may be more effective when combined with economic incentives and the control of working conditions for professional drivers. The education of the young at school can increase awareness of accident and environmental hazards.

Transport and traffic management

National level

Outline laws define general objectives and describe the basic means of action – investment, pricing and regulation – in the transport sector. This is the level at which links can occur between sub-sector policies, such as the policy with respect to the roads in the national network, road safety policy, and also the policies which relate to other sectors such as the environment or regional planning. Measures deal with the construction of new infrastructure and lay down the rules which govern the operation and pricing of existing infrastructure.

At the national level, the pricing of infrastructure and the nature of the investments which are offered (combined transport, for example) may influence users and companies to choose modes of transport which provide greater or lesser safety while being more or less damaging to the environment. Other policies, such as the budget that establishes tax levels, for example on fuel, dominate transportation and limit the areas where action is possible.

There is agreement amongst experts on the need for a return to realistic pricing for road, rail, air and river transport by internalising pricing in order to halt the increase in road transport. New systems of taxation that help to achieve this have been introduced in Northern Europe. The long awaited environmental tax on energy or CO_2 in transport demands supranational harmonisation so that it does not harm the competitiveness of economies. However, doubts have been raised in regard of the effectiveness of internalising pricing :

> "Moves towards life-cycle analysis, full-cost accounting, and full-cost pricing are desirable components of strategies for achieving sustainable transportation. However, full-cost pricing may not be enough to secure sustainability; even higher prices may have to be imposed, or other measures" (9).

The development of motorways and four-lane dual carriageways has resulted in greater traffic flow and reduced accident risk. The development of rail-road combined transport system can help reduce both pollution and the very severe accidents which result from lorries using the roads. The decisions to construct major infrastructure increasingly involved standardised appraisal and consultation procedures which consider both road safety and environmental protection.

Finally, national traffic restrictions relating to certain categories of vehicles on certain networks at certain periods (lorries in Austria at night-time, for example) also provide an example of measures which combine road safety and environmental objectives. It is however necessary to evaluate the negative effects caused by traffic transfer resulting from such a measure (transfer to the daytime in the case of Austria).

Local level

At the local level, a large number of authorities have introduced measures for traffic or urban travel plans such as the following:

- Regulation by introducing standards for density and zoning, by providing parking spaces at places of residence and firms as well as public car parks, by limiting speeds in areas with traffic calming (30 km/h) and on the road system (50 km/h), by traffic restraint, parking restrictions and delivery restrictions on a spatial basis (inner city, zones, street, or lane) or on a temporal basis (night-time, peak period) for different modes,

- Installing a traffic management system,

- Developing a system of streets and roads (by-passes, roundabouts), organising road sharing systems (cycle tracks, priority bus lanes) and intermodal co-ordination by means of park and ride facilities and freight terminals, investing in public transport,

- Imposing urban tolls, parking charges and subsidising public transport.

When the objective is solely to reduce congestion (which is frequently the case), the effects on the environment and safety are not always positive, because CO and HC emissions are reduced, but increased vehicle speeds reduce road safety and increases NO_x and noise emissions. As well, traffic becomes dispersed over the urban space and over time, which is prejudicial to peace and safety.

On the other hand, the implementation of a traffic restraint plan (traffic calming, 30 km/h zone, etc.) has positive consequences for both safety and the environment, but raises the problem of the transfer of traffic to other streets and zones and the lengthening of travel distances. Speed limits become more effective when they are accompanied by modifications to the road and its surroundings. Restrictions on deliveries and parking are generally effective in that they reduce travel and increase traffic safety. Street-side parking is a source of danger (masking of pedestrians) but is also positive in that it limits speeds by reducing the amount of available space. By-passes around urban areas are beneficial from the point of view of safety and the environment by reducing motorised through traffic. However, they are detrimental due to increased risk at points where other roads intersect with the by-pass and because they harm the landscape and result in poorer air quality in the outskirts, particularly in the absence of measures which regulate land use and construction in the new perimeter served by the by-pass.

The promotion of walking or bicycle use by restricting car use should be accompanied by safety measures. The strategies which are chosen in order to prevent two-wheeled vehicle accidents should take account of the type of road, the traffic and the urban environment, for example: separation of flows with cycle lanes, that take account of problems associated with intersections and priority bus lanes; transfer to footpaths, addressing the problem of conflict with pedestrians; or mixed traffic with speed limits. All other measures which aim to dissuade motorists from using their cars by making public transport attractive (quality of service, pricing, park and ride) are beneficial.

Major road infrastructure

There is a general tendency, in both urban and rural areas, to revise the standards for roads in order to lay down a new functional hierarchy for traffic lanes which integrates the safety concerns of all types of road users (10). In urban areas, there is no longer any reluctance to reduce capacity and level of service in order to improve safety. The phenomenon of risk compensation should be taken into consideration when the quality of the road along a route is improved. The gains which accrue from safety improvements (surface, geometric design, road markings, safety barriers) are often used by road users to increase speeds. The same type of law applies here as in the case of congestion, where any gain in traffic flow which results from an increase in capacity or improved traffic management is cancelled out by an increase in travel.

This is probably the area in which there are the greatest number of conflicts and convergences between road safety and environmental protection.

Examples of conflicts:

- Roundabouts. These improve traffic flow and safety. However, a contribution from town planners and landscape architects is required in order to integrate them within the urban fabric.

- Roadside trees: when too close to the carriageway these are fatal obstacles for a car which leaves the road. If such trees are in the immediate vicinity of the carriageway, safety barriers should be installed. Lacking barriers, such trees should be cut down and replanted or moved on the grounds of safety.

- Noise barriers can create severance effects or visual intrusion for residents.

- Fencing along motorways creates a severance effect for animals. This means that crossing structures must be installed.

- Salting of roads improves winter traffic and safety conditions, but may be harmful to soil and water.

Examples of convergence:

- Integration with the landscape makes it possible to discover and remodel the landscape. It also improves the visual comfort of road users, which results in lower levels of stress and improved safety while driving.

- In the treatment of motorway rest areas; the provision of an embankment protects sleeping lorry drivers from disturbance. Currently, in addition to service areas, rest areas and even discovery areas are also created. There is convergence here between safety and landscaping.

- The use of porous asphalt on motorways increases safety (rapid drainage of surface water during rain) and leads to a noticeable reduction in vehicle noise. It does, however, appear that such pavements may cause motorists to increase their speeds.

- The speed limits which apply on different types of road are also a link between road safety and the environment.

Table II.3 suggests a qualitative appraisal of situations of conflict and/or convergence between road safety and the environment on the basis of the different types of measures which are possible with respect to road vehicles, travel demand management policies, infrastructure and traffic management. For many of these measures, the quality of the outcome is highly dependent on design.

A high degree of convergence of objectives is reached if all the effects are positive for a given measure, as applies in the case of vehicle checks, access restrictions and traffic calming. Conversely, conflicts become apparent when, for a given measure, the effects are positive in one respect and negative in another, as is the case with some road improvements. The introduction of taxes on vehicles and fuel in order to reduce trip-making and re-establish competition between modes can only be beneficial to safety.

Social communication and administrative management are important as a means of informing the public about the basis of the policies which have been decided. The publication of a list of vehicles with information about their performance and respective costs will affect the choices which consumers make when they purchase or replace a vehicle.

Table II.3. **Examples of conflicts and convergences between road safety and environment**

		Energy conservation	CO_2 reduction	Air quality	Noise reduction	Landscape	Safety
Road vehicles	Vehicle weight reductions	+	+	=	?	=	-
	Power reductions	+	+	+	?	=	+
	Limiting maximum speeds	+	+	+	+	=	+
	Electric vehicle	?	+/-	+	+	=	+/-
	Vehicle checks	+	+	+	+	=	+
	Driver training	+	+	+	+	+	+
Transport	Transfer to rail	+	+	+	+	+/-	+
	Intermodal transport in urban areas	+	+	+	+	=	-
Road infrastructure	Roundabouts	?	?	?	?	-	+
	By-passes	+/-	+/-	+	+/-	-	+
	Noise barriers	=	=	+	+	-	+
	Porous asphalt	=	=	=	+	=	+/-
	De-icing salts	?	=	=	-	-	+/-
Traffic	Reduction in speed limit	+	+	+	+	=	+
	Control of speeds	+	+	+	+	=	+
	Traffic calming	+/-	+/-	=/+	+	+	+
	Access restrictions	+	+	+	+	+	+
	Congestion management	+	+	+	-	=	-

Note:
- \+ positive effect as regards objective
- = no effect as regards objective
- \- negative effect as regards objective
- +/- effect may be either way
- ? uncertain effect

Land use

Present transport system development has had a severe impact on urban structure and cities. As reported by the OECD/ECMT report (2), the increase of car travel and goods transport by road,

"was once expected to level out at a point where, given reasonable investment, roads could be provided to accommodate for it. While many small towns have been, and still are, able to cope with the traffic they generate, the much higher volumes found in cities are less easily handled. It is possible that they could be accommodated by dispersing city-centre activities and embarking on sustained road investment programmes, as many American cities have done, but, this would have huge costs associated with it, serious resource and environmental implications and no guarantee of eliminating congestion".

Urban areas are affected by several processes that increase travel demand. To some extent, these processes, in their turn, are caused by the development of the transport system, especially the role of the passenger car. An early trend, initiated by the metropolitan rail and tram networks in the 19th century, was the move to the suburbs. Later on, the increasing shift of housing has emptied city centres of inhabitants and left severely depressed areas around many large centres.

Other more recent trends are the dispersion of employment towards the urban fringes, and the large-scale concentration of commercial activity in edge city "hypermarkets". Urban sprawl, caused by very low density development, is intensified by these edge city developments, which at the same time demand an ever more complex network of streets and highways. City centres are further weakened and edge areas are fragmented into developments of intense activity, interspersed with under-utilised or environmentally decayed areas.

Trips to work, for shopping and leisure grow ever longer and public transport opportunities decline as people and activities are spread ever thinner. But travel pattern studies show that travel and traffic conditions in different cities are not uniform. Increases in trip length are very unevenly distributed and there is great variation in the travel mode mix. There is an extensive choice of measures to protect the environment, or improve environmental quality, as already shown in, for instance, a study on road traffic and the environment (11):

- General traffic management schemes, which may have other objectives, can also improve the environment, provided that they:

  - maintain a human scale;
  - do not exceed the environmental capacity of the streets in the area;
  - are compatible with other urban planning policies;
  - consider and provide for the needs of public transport;
  - segregate car, public transport, lorry, cycle and pedestrian routes where this is beneficial;
  - consider giving priority to access on foot and by bicycle;
  - limit access by car to the periphery of main shopping areas;
  - reduce through traffic;
  - remove non-essential car parking ;
  - avoid major new construction and street widening;

- control speed and use landscaping features to enhance the character of the road, and discourage through traffic;

- co-ordinate signal controlled junctions to allow continuous traffic flow and reduce noise caused by the stopping and starting of vehicles;

- use coloured and textured surfaces, street furniture, vegetation, water features, seating and shelter to enhance the visual appearance of the street scene;

- maintain high standards of maintenance and reinstatement to help reduce noise and vibration.

- Traffic management schemes may also be designed to reinforce planning measures and improve the environment. Examples of these schemes include: management schemes and the licensing of lorry depots subject to consideration of amenity and environmental factors; pedestrianisation; residential streets on the lines of the "woonerven" system used in the Netherlands; and reorganising parking.

- Other measures that minimise environmental disturbance where it cannot be avoided include for instance: providing noise insulation for buildings; landscaping, screening and planting to minimise noise and visual intrusion; and careful siting and design of traffic control equipment and signs.

Change, fluidity and variation are characteristics of vital towns and cities. As economic and social structures change, areas allowing a productive mix of functions, such as city centres, can maintain a flexible response to the changes, while functionally segregated areas may lose the basis of their existence (12). One aspect of vitality is that growth and improvement in some areas is accompanied by decay in others. No strategy can provide a permanently beautiful or healthy city, but there are always means and measures that can be used to influence the processes of change. When, as now, urban travel has proved to be a central problem, the measures available are those of co-ordinated land use planning and transport policy. In the OECD/ECMT report (2) on urban travel and sustainable development, they are listed as follows:

a) Land-use planning and development control policies that influence settlement patterns and increase the accessibility to jobs, shops and other facilities, without the need to travel by car;

b) Policies affecting the pricing of fuel, car purchase and licensing, parking and road use to influence vehicle design, the location of activities, modal choice and the growth of teleworking;

c) Measures making use of telematics to integrate signal control, parking and public transport management to raise the efficiency of the urban travel system and promote shifts from cars to other modes;

d) Policies making employers responsible for commuter planning to reduce peak traffic flows;

e) Policies concerning subsidy, privatisation and the use of upgraded information systems and marketing to increase the efficiency and attractiveness of public transport;

f) Measures to set up car-free zones, traffic calming and cycle and pedestrian priority to assist pedestrians and cyclists, reduce the risks to these modes, and improve the attractiveness of cities;

g) Measures to promote goods trans-shipment depots and city-friendly delivery vans to suit logistics to urban conditions.

Measures under this heading are, naturally, very often the same ones that have been dealt with earlier in regard to transport and traffic management and they have the same implications for possible conflict and convergence of their environmental and traffic safety impacts.

Measures to halt urban sprawl such as increasing residential density around central areas or reinstating shopping malls in city centres, while contributing to a reduction in travel demand, also concentrate people and trip-generating facilities in zones where present traffic loads may already be considerable. A similar outcome may result when applying measures to promote mixed land use, such as placing businesses and enterprises in residential areas.

II.6. REFERENCES

1.   BROWN, I.D. (1992). *Conflicts between mobility, safety and environmental preservation expressed as a hierarchy of social dilemmas.* IATSS, 16, 2, 124-128. Tokyo.

2.   OECD/ECMT (1995*). Urban travel and sustainable development.* OECD, Paris.

3.   OECD. ROAD TRANSPORT RESEARCH (1984). *Integrated road safety programmes.* OECD, Paris.

4.   OECD. ROAD TRANSPORT RESEARCH (1990). *Integrated traffic safety management in urban areas.* OECD, Paris.

5.   CAMPBELL, B.J. (1992). *Safety versus mobility.* IATSS, 16.2. 149-156. IATSS, Tokyo.

6.   IWW, INFRAS (1995). *External effects of transports,* Project for UIC Paris, Final report.

7.   MENY, Y. and J.C. THOENIG (1989). *Politiques publiques.* Presses Universitaires de France, Paris.

8.   LINDBERG, G. (1994). *Quantitative methods on environmental impact assessment on programmes and projects of land transport: practices in Sweden / Les méthodes quantitatives d'évaluation de l'impact sur l'environnement des programmes et projets de transports terrestres.* Actes INRETS n°41. INRETS, Arcueil.

9.   OECD. Environment Directorate (1997). *Towards Sustainable Transportation,* Proceedings of the International Conference, organised by the OECD and hosted by the Government of Canada, Vancouver, British Columbia, 24-27 March 1996, OECD, Paris.

10.   KOORNSTRA, M.J. (1994). *The Dutch policy for sustainable road safety.* Paper for the advanced studies Institute: transport, environment and road safety. Tinbergen Institute. SWOV, Leidschendam.

11.   WILLIAMS, M., B. HEDGES and E. FERNANDO (1978). *Road Traffic and the Environment.* Social and Community Planning Research. London

12.   MORRIS, W. and J.A. KAUFMAN (1996). *Mixed use development, designs to reduce travel and generate employment.* Proceedings of the 24th European Transport Forum, Seminar B. PTRC Education and Research Services Ltd, London.

13.   OECD. ROAD TRANSPORT RESEARCH (1994). *Congestion Control and Demand Management.* OECD, Paris.

14.   OECD. ROAD TRANSPORT RESEARCH (1977). *Safety of Vulnerable Road Users.* OECD, Paris.

CHAPTER III   REVIEW OF INDICATORS AND EVALUATION FRAMEWORKS

The context and benefits of integration of safety and environmental issues were described in Chapter II. However, it is necessary to have appropriate methodologies in place that make integration possible. This chapter contains a review of the methods currently in use and pays particular attention to the indicators that appear to be most appropriate for safety and environmental integration.

The OECD Group on "the state of the environment" devoted part of its work programme to the development of indicators for the integration of environmental concerns into transport policies. Where appropriate this report also makes use of this work. More detail and examples from different countries are available in the OECD Environment Monograph (15).

Measurements of the individual effects of problems or nuisances are discussed in this report in relation to:

- **Indicators,** i.e. tools of measurement;

and the ways of combining them are referred to as:

- **Evaluation frameworks** which are used as means of valuing disadvantages or costs and benefits in some common way so that they can be compared and, where there is conflict, weighed one against the other.

III.1. INDICATORS

Indicators need to be reliable, readable, measurable, policy relevant, and acceptable to politicians and the public. However, there is no universal set of indicators available, but rather several sets which meet the needs of specific conceptual frameworks and purposes. For example, those indicators which are used to evaluate local projects may well be different from those used at the national or international level.   The main indicators of particular relevance to safety and environmental integration are presented in Table III.1.

Indicators are needed to measure both:

- The *incidence* of the problem, e.g. the amount of noise, the amount of traffic, the number of accidents, the quality of the air, and

- The *impact* on people's lives, e.g. number of casualties, amount of ill health, the number of days off work/in hospital for related illnesses, the amount of discomfort or nuisance.

Table III.1. **Key indicators for integrating safety and environmental aspects**

Indicator Classification	Indicator
Road and Traffic	Total vehicle-kilometres
	Volume of road traffic per unit of GDP or per capita
	Person-kilometres and tonne-kilometres
	Average speed
	Annual average daily traffic
	Length and density of the road network
	Modal split
Risk and Safety	Casualties
	Severity
	Monetary cost
	Accidents per million vehicle-kilometres
	Public perception
	Target achievment
Environmental Impact	Noise
	Vibration
	Air pollution
	Energy consumption
	Barrier effect and community severance
	Visual intrusion
	Disruption during construction
	Water pollution
	Biological diversity, flora and fauna
	Cultural heritage and landscape values
	Other environmental impacts
Instruments	Taxation and subsidies
	Price structure - fuel use, road use
Process (co-operation in institutions, management)	Degree of co-operation between different actors
	Quality and number of local integrated safety/environmental programmes
	Competence levels and motivational aspects

When suitable indicators of the individual effects have been developed, it is then necessary to be able to combine the indicators of the individual factors in some way, so that an overall effect of a particular project or policy can be calculated to assist in decision making. However, it is rare for decisions to be made mechanistically in this way, and the evaluation frameworks generally only guide or advise decision makers. This is discussed more fully later.

The following levels of measurement are common:

- measurement in physical units
- quantification in monetary value
- subjective ratings

The type of impact, the degree of impact and how extensive in terms of area affected or number of people affected are also relevant considerations. The rate (microgrammes per vehicle km or accidents per vehicle km), the total (tonnes or accidents per year) and quality or severity of the impact are also important aspects. Exposure is an important factor to consider especially when dealing with vulnerable road users such as children or the elderly.

Intermediate or surrogate measures are also used. Speed, traffic composition or traffic volume may be used instead of accidents; emissions instead of air quality; or even traffic flow to predict emissions to predict air quality. Use of surrogate measures is often taken to a more sophisticated level by making use of mathematical modelling using a number of variables to predict effects. The prediction equations developed can then be used to provide standard assessment tables for various impacts from the levels of the predictive variables, for example to predict noise or emissions of particular pollutants, from a particular traffic flow and mix of vehicles.

Prediction methods for accidents, air pollution and noise have been the subject of extensive research and are now well developed (2, 17). The models are used for post evaluation of projects as well as predictions for new projects.

A lot of effort has been made to assign monetary values to the various impacts, but this has proved more difficult for environmental factors than some others. Though it is currently not feasable, in the future it may be possible to make a monetary estimate of the costs and the value of all the impacts and benefits. This aspect is dealt with further in the section on evaluation frameworks.

III.1.1. *Road and traffic indicators*

Traffic

Trends in road traffic are fundamental determinants of pressure on the environment and traffic flow volumes are also often related to safety. As well, two principal functions of traffic can be distinguished: goods transport and passenger transport. For both the following could be measured (15) to reveail trends:

- total vehicle kilometres (average annual distance covered, multiplied by the number of vehicles in operation);
- volume of road traffic per unit of GDP;
- volume of road traffic per capita.

It may also be relevant to consider person-kilometres and tonne-kilometres (goods). Moreover, these indicators can be further nuanced to distinguish levels of travel benefit (persons) or profitability/productivity (goods). This notion is more easily quantified in the latter case, where monetary values are known per unit weight or volume of the goods transported. For example, a tonne of coals justifies lower costs per vehicle-kilometre than a tonne of computer circuit boards.

In the case of passenger travel, benefits are often crudely assumed to be higher for travel associated with economic activity, notably travel to and from employment. Travellers may not share this assumption, often valuing travel for family and recreational activities as much as, or more than, work-related travel (21).

In the same way that efforts are made to measure the perceived value of environmental and safety consequences – including such intangibles and semi-tangibles as visual blight or pain and suffering – indicators may be developed to reflect the perceived benefits of alternative ways to "consume" person-kilometres in motor vehicles.

For local impacts, traffic flow, commonly measured in terms of annual average daily traffic (3) is used, possibly together with speed where the average speed and 85th percentile speeds are used. Data availability and quality can be good if use is made of modern technology for detecting vehicles, but a reasonable sample of sites and regular counts are required. Interview surveys and the keeping of diaries by a representative sample of the population can give good information on travel patterns and modal choice.

Road network length/density

The length of the road network is an indicator of the development of transport infrastructure, which in turn is an important component of transport supply, and is therefore relevant to both environmental effects and safety.

The density of the road network can provide a rough indication of the space that is consumed by road infrastructure. Trends can be measured by using a base year as an index.

III.1.2. Safety Indicators

Indicators for safety are reasonably well established, although there are a number of options and differences of opinion as to what should be used. The examples described below could also be referred to as danger indicators. Some countries use of positive safety indicators such as the use of seat belt, child seats, and others. Sweden is a good example of a country that uses this approach.

Casualties

The most common measure of safety is the number of casualties, although sometimes the number of injury accidents is a preferred measure. Both depend on a reliable accident reporting system and good quality accident database. This varies from country to country and never achieves inclusion of all accidents.

With good data, experience of the effect of policies and treatments can be built up and the number of accidents, related to new projects, can be accurately estimated. A particular difficulty that is encountered with local schemes is the small numbers of accidents and thus the problem of achieving statistically significant information. Attempts are sometimes made to improve the injury accident information by using hospital admissions data and damage only accidents. Hospital data has been shown to be more accurate for some types of accident – e.g. cycling – that are not reported to the police.

Damage only accidents could provide a much larger number of occurrences and therefore more reliable statistical data. Unfortunately, the reporting of such data is usually poor.

Severity

The different overall degrees of severity of injuries – numbers which are fatal, serious or slight – are relevant in terms of safety benefits. A severity ratio – the number of accidents which are fatal or serious, as a proportion of total accidents – is used as an indicator of severity. At the national level, the number killed is an appropriate indicator of safety, but at the local level the small number of fatalities would provide an unreliable indicator.

Definition of the different severity levels can also be problematical as is the problem of under-reporting of accidents, and the possible variation in reporting rates for a variety of reasons, e.g. insurance claims. The latter is probably more of relevance for slight injuries.

Road User Groups

Casualties in different road user groups can also be considered separately, often with a particular emphasis on the effect on vulnerable road users (pedestrians and cyclists).

Monetary cost of accidents

Some countries put a monetary value on accidents and casualties (22). The monetary benefit of the numbers of accidents saved by a particular project can then be calculated and used in cost-benefit analysis.

Monetary values can be assigned to different types of accident. The average value used may be derived using the "willingness to pay" method. This assesses what people would be prepared to pay to reduce the risk to them of an accident. The responses are then averaged to determine the cost to save one statistical life. An additional allowance is included for other economic resource costs such as medical costs and damage to vehicles. Another method, now less favoured, is based on the human capital approach, which places a value on the gross contribution the individual casualty would have made to the economy, plus an allowance for pain, grief and suffering, police, insurance and administration costs. Values are available for different classes of road user, related to the severity of injury likely to be suffered by different road user groups (4). Urban and rural accidents can also be costed separately, as can the different severities of casualties.

Where countries have made such monetary valuations, they do vary from country to country a good deal (6), which perhaps calls into question the robustness of the approach.

Intermediate indicators/proxies for accidents

Because of the small numbers of accidents at any one location, and their variability, proxy measures are sometimes used instead of accident or casualty numbers. The most common are speed, conflicts or traffic flow. Research has shown good relationships between these more readily measurable factors, and accidents (7). A reduction in these is considered to indicate an improvement in safety. More sophisticated prediction equations are now also available for particular types of junction and links or even whole networks. These equations can be used to estimate the safety benefits of schemes (17).

Risk

Using the number of accidents as an indicator of safety takes no account of the amount of travel or the increase in traffic flow. It is therefore common to use an accident rate, expressed in terms of the number of accidents/casualties per distance travelled, time travelled, or per journey or per capita. It is common to use "accidents per million vehicle kilometres" to give a rate, as opposed to "accidents per year" which gives the incidence of the problem. But there is some dispute as to whether using a rate is a valid indicator of safety, particularly if the number of accidents increases due to generated traffic. Improvement in risk means that travel is safer, but the community may not be.

Subjective indicators

Accident numbers are not always as convincing to the public as are subjective indicators of safety. It is often said that dangerous locations have few accidents because people will not expose themselves to risk in these locations. In such situations a subjective measure of public perceptions of danger, measured via social surveys, may be a more appropriate indicator.

Targets

Rather than using absolute numbers of accidents, projects may also be rated as to how much they will contribute towards a target. A number of countries have adopted accident reduction targets (23) for a given year and projects and policies are examined in relation to the contribution they make towards achieving this target. Targets may be national or local, and are often simply phrased as a percentage reduction by a certain date. But targets in isolation may be problematic for integration as they may result in conflicting approaches. There is therefore a case for integrated /joint safety environmental targets to be set.

III.1.3.   Environmental impact indicators

Noise

Road traffic noise (24) is a principal cause of the perception of noise as a nuisance. Numerous research projects (9) indicate that an outdoor level of 65 dB L_{Aeq} is unacceptable and an outdoor level of less than 55 dB is desirable. More recently the World Health Organisation has suggested (18) that to protect the majority of people from being moderately annoyed during the daytime, noise should not exceed 55 L_{Aeq} and at night time 45 L_{Aeq}.

Noise measurement methods applicable to assessing the benefits of different traffic projects can be divided into two categories:

- traffic noise measurements, and.
- vehicle noise measurements.

Traffic noise at a given location is the combined noise from individual vehicles in a traffic stream. In assessing the impact of traffic noise on the environment, two scales for describing traffic noise levels have been developed which have been found to correlate reasonably well with people's dissatisfaction with road traffic noise experienced in their homes.

The first scale, L_{Aeq}, is widely used in European countries and the USA. It is concerned with the energy content of the noise. The alternative scale, L_{A10}, focuses on the statistical variability of the fluctuating noise level that is exceeded for 10 per cent of the time (1). This scale is used in UK for environmental assessment purposes for new road schemes (3). Although these two scales are very different in describing traffic noise, surveys have shown that for the majority of situations of practical interest there is a direct linear correspondence between the two scales with L_{A10} generally exceeding L_{Aeq} by about 3dB.

A method for measuring individual vehicle noise can also be used to estimate traffic noise levels (8). The method requires the measurement of both noise levels and speeds of a representative sample of vehicles as they pass a point near the road. The information gained from this measurement can be used to obtain a noise level for any given speed for each different category of vehicle. This type of measurement can be used to compare noise levels at different sites, for a variety of traffic flows, compositions or speed. For example, it can be used to determine changes in noise before and after the introduction of traffic management or traffic calming schemes where speed changes may have occurred (1).

Instead of noise measurements, subjective rating scales of public perception of noise nuisance can be used. Studies have, however, shown that perception of noise nuisance is more susceptible to changes than to absolute levels (9). The number/percentage of people exposed or disturbed is also important as an indicator, either at the level to severely disturb sleep and communication and thereby contribute to health problems, or at the level of causing a nuisance. Ambient noise relative to the type of environment or land use affected should also be considered.

Some countries use monetary values of noise nuisance, based on a variety of techniques, but it has been difficult to arrive at convincing values as the evidence for monetary values of the effect of noise has been complex and at times conflicting.

Noise is one of the environmental factors that can conflict with safety, e.g. some traffic calming schemes may increase noise if there is a large proportion of lorries in the flow. In other situations, convergence of noise and safety benefits may occur, e.g. when total traffic flows are reduced, so methods of comparative evaluation, e.g. monetary values may be helpful. Another technique in evaluation is to use the cost of reducing a particular noise problem rather than putting a cost on the particular noise level.

Vibration

Traffic induced vibrations in buildings are normally measured by geophones or accelerometers attached to a wall, floor or window. In addition, the propagation of ground vibration from the roadside to buildings requires further measurements, often taken at the edge of the road and at relevant building foundations, using geophones attached rigidly to the structure.

Measurement of low frequency noise is simpler and with the correct equipment can be carried out simultaneously with traffic noise measurements. Low frequency noise levels in the range of 20-200 Hz can normally be determined using simple hand held instrumentation. More sophisticated equipment allows sound pressure levels at different frequencies to be measured (11).

Air pollution

Many countries have limit values for different exhaust emission pollutants which are considered harmful. Proposals have been agreed in some countries for the establishment of national standards using a "base standard" and "alert threshold".

Nationally grammes per person per day, annual tonnes or microgrammes per vehicle kilometre of particular pollutants, are common indicators (15). Locally indicators for the assessment of the level of air pollution are generally tackled in three ways:

- measuring air quality
- measuring emissions from vehicles
- modelling emissions from traffic data

The significance of air pollution is normally assessed in terms of the average concentration over a certain time period. Specific criteria for different compounds depend on the mechanism of their environmental impact. Typical examples with reference to human health impacts are hydrocarbons, whose action on the body is cumulative, and carbon monoxide, which reacts quickly and reversibly with haemoglobin to reduce the blood's oxygen carrying capacity. In the first case, exposure over extended periods is of importance, and standards are expressed normally as annual mean values, while in the second case, short term exposures can be significant so standards limit 8-hour or shorter average concentrations. There are also pollutants whose local concentrations are unimportant, their effects depending on the total amount present in the atmosphere. Greenhouse gases, such as carbon dioxide, are of this type, and their environmental effects are usually evaluated from estimates of total emissions.

There is an immense number of techniques and principles for measuring quality. Many are well established. Any difficulties are not because of the analytical process but relate to the design of a measurement programme and the interpretation of results. Any change must be very large for it to be detected with confidence (2). The implication of this is that air pollution monitoring needs to be extensive if its results are to be used to distinguish between different situations and then to predict for new situations. Unfortunately, the amount of air pollution monitoring that can be carried out is severely limited by cost.

Measurement and modelling of emissions from vehicles has generally been done by either laboratory tests or on road tests of samples of vehicles in different conditions. Results can then be used to calculate total emissions from a particular traffic flow, but so far such models are based on crude averages. More precise modelling is difficult as vehicle emission rates are inherently variable – tests on different vehicles of the same type may differ by a factor of ten. How hot or cold the engine is also needs to be taken into account, especially for vehicles with catalytic converters. It is therefore necessary to have extensive amounts of data in order to provide a good representative understanding of the emission characteristics of road vehicles.

Where concentrations are to be estimated, the dispersion of the emissions must also be modelled, taking into account the weather conditions and other local or regional influences. In addition, for pollutants that are chemically active, their atmospheric transformations must be considered. Currently there is a lack of information on dispersion rates, although research is being undertaken.

Some early attempts have been made to assign monetary values to air pollution (6) but this is likely to be a difficult area to obtain acceptable monetary evaluations. The response in a "Willingness to Accept" approach provides a monetary compensation for a given loss in environmental quality that is typically several times higher than the amount of the same respondents' "Willingness to Pay" for an equivalent level of environmental improvement. Moreover, this difference appears much larger than can be accounted for by wealth effects (19). The strength of this asymmetry may vary with the environmental issue under consideration.

Measuring the number of people affected is relevant in any assessment of schemes including specific groups affected – e.g. children, asthmatics.

Air pollution indicators which relate to integration with safety will generally be at the local level – traffic management schemes, etc. At the regional or global level an overall reduction in vehicle usage may affect both safety and environment (13).

Energy consumption

Energy consumption indicators are generally based on vehicle performance or national sales of fuel. Joules are the unit of measurement. The composition of the vehicle fleet is relevant in any calculations, particularly age and engine size. Sample survey data is also widely used. Energy consumption is relevant to air pollution but probably less relevant for integration with safety.

Barrier effect and community severance

Methods of measuring barrier effects and community severance in relation to people's movements have not been fully established or validated, although research has been done (1).

A measure of the number at risk of severance by a road scheme can be made by first defining target locations – shops, post offices etc. – and then mapping their catchment areas. The populations potentially affected by severance can be estimated from the dwellings in the portion of the catchment severed from the facility by the scheme, using geographical data bases or survey data to infer the number of users of the facility. Surveys of the population potentially affected can also be used to identify routes threatened by severance, especially those that do not have clearly defined catchment areas, such as routes and tracks used for recreation and leisure. Relative severity can be expressed either by the number of people affected, the amount of trips suppressed, or the length of detours.

Community severance may also be caused by construction or traffic management schemes changing the traffic characteristics on existing roads or streets, or increasing traffic disturbance in the immediate vicinity of an area, even if no paths or routes are cut.

In urban area projects, barrier effects and community severance are always one of the main public concerns where the debate will generally focus on any severance not taken into account in design. There is little use of monetary evaluation of barrier effects. One example is the Danish Highway Investment Model, using 50 per cent of noise costs for barrier effects (12).

Visual intrusion

For assessing the visual impact of a road, mathematical techniques using the angle of incidence have been developed, but the assessment is generally based on subjective evaluation of the impact, taking into account the type of landscape and number of people affected within a surrounding visual envelope (3). In urban areas and areas with especially sensitive landscapes, visual intrusion is always a central theme of debate, and evaluation will often be expressed less through formal techniques and more in the development of public opinion. Improved visualisation methods create detailed before-and-after illustrations even at relatively early stages of design. These can also be extended to simulation models, allowing an experience of moving along the road in a traffic situation or looking at the road from different stationary or moving viewpoints.

Disruption during construction

Indicators for disruption during construction can be based on the type of impacts, scale of works, and number of people affected.

Water pollution

Indicators have been developed regarding the risks of pollution of groundwater or watercourses, relating these risks mainly to the frequency of hazardous transport, accident frequency, spill risks, run-off levels and characteristics of the terrain. Similar indicators have been used to assess risks from de-icing salt use. Extensive research is under way, especially in the USA, into the construction risks to water quality, aquatic flora and fauna. The research focuses on the construction of such things as embankments, bridges, drainage or non-permeable surfacing, and how such construction changes the characteristics of the catchment area or flows in all kinds of wetlands and coastal areas.

Biological diversity, flora and fauna

Traditionally, impacts on fauna have been expressed as road kills or, for large animals, crash risks. Assessment of impacts on flora have centred on possible risks associated with the destruction sensitive habitats. As the importance of protecting biological diversity has come to the fore, research has been directed to impacts on animal and plant populations. A basic indicator of risk, especially to endangered species, is loss and fragmentation of natural habitats and loss of paths between habitats. There is, however, a lack of data on the long-term impacts of different degrees of severity of fragmentation and on the effect of such mitigation measures as ecoducts and green bridges.

A risk that is not presently assessed on a general basis concerns the changes in migration conditions and possible foreign species introduced as a consequence of an infrastructure construction project. Vegetation introduced for landscaping and species spreading along, for instance, a major highway, may affect native populations.

Cultural heritage and landscape values

Nationally and regionally important areas and objects related to cultural heritage, as well as valuable landscape areas, have usually been listed in registers and are the object of legally mandated protection. Locally important areas and objects can be identified in plans or inventories, but are not always legally protected. The seriousness of impact is primarily determined by whether any protected objects or areas are concerned. For large-scale schemes, a count of the potential conflicts (for instance a road crossing an area or in its immediate vicinity) will give early-stage information on the seriousness (20).

Other environmental impacts

In many countries, land take – the amount of land needed for a project – is a fundamental indicator of environmental impact. Land take can for instance be classified according to the cultural, natural or landscape values of the land. It can also be classified by uses for other purposes, such as construction, recreation or agriculture.

Geological risks – i.e. risks to soil quality and to agricultural land – are generally assessed in relation to the size and quality of the area at risk.

For social and socio-economic impacts, indicators have not been developed for general use though research has been conducted in many countries. Some social impacts are expressed through barrier effects.

Planning blight – i.e. the impact on communities affected by typically very long planning processes, falling property values, difficulty in selling properties, falling investment and maintenance – is usually not expressed by indicators. However, methods of measuring with the help of maintenance cost comparisons and extra resource cost identification have been suggested (6).

III.2. EVALUATION FRAMEWORKS

Many countries currently use a systematic method for evaluation and prioritisation of road infrastructure projects (14), but there is a great variation in the extent and methods used. For major new projects, sophisticated integrated methods are often used, but for many other projects, environmental issues and road safety are often treated separately, if at all.

The most commonly used methods that are employed for identifying the impacts of a project are cost-benefit analysis and multi-criteria analysis. There are also simple approaches such as matrices, interaction diagrams and check lists that can be used.

Cost-benefit analysis

Cost-benefit analysis tries to take account of all the welfare benefits of a particular intervention. A project is deemed desirable if the benefits are in excess of the estimated costs. Different economic indices are used to aggregate costs and benefits into a single value which reflects the profitability of the project. The index used can be Net Present Value, Internal Rate of Return, Benefit- Cost Ratio, or First Year Rate of Return (6). The detailed methods and values used vary considerably between countries which adopt this approach. There are differences in the effects which are given a monetary value and in the monetary value applied.

Multi-criteria analysis

Multi-criteria analysis uses both the effects which have been given a monetary value and all other effects considered to be of interest. The latter are measured in non monetary terms, often subjectively scaled. Values for all factors, whether money or not, are then weighted so that an overall assessment can be calculated. The overall score for a project is calculated by summing the product of ratings and weights across all criteria. Rank order for projects can be compared using different weights (sensitivity analysis). Weights are generally derived using interview surveys with experts or the public.

A mixture of both techniques

Some countries use a mixture of both cost-benefit and multi-criteria methods. Cost-benefit analysis is taken as far as reasonably possible to give, for example, a net present value. The NPV is then supplemented by a framework of the unquantifiable (in money terms) effects which are described in words or rated on a scale.

Matrices, Interaction Diagrams and Check lists

These simpler approaches can be used to identify what possible significant impacts can be expected, without necessitating calculation or other exact predictions of the magnitude of the impacts.

Comparison of the different approaches

The cost-benefit approach has the advantage that it summarises effects into a single value, which makes it easy to compare different options. Its weakness is that effects which cannot be valued in money terms have to be excluded and even those that are valued in money terms may have a dubious value put on them. Monetary evaluation of environmental impacts is difficult to achieve because the evaluation of environmental effects cannot be easily related to the market system. The attitude and use of monetary valuation of environmental and safety impacts differ greatly from country to country.

The need for monetary evaluation and aggregation was mainly developed for the purpose of programme planning, but uncertainty will always exist in the estimation and valuation of long term cumulative and global effects. It is then necessary to admit that all effects cannot be included in cost-benefit analysis, but rather the most significant effects must be selected and used (14).

While in theory cost-benefit analysis should improve the basis for decision making by providing a common unit of value and indicating the efficiency of resource usage, studies have shown that no correlation existed between cost-benefit ratios and those schemes actually adopted, (16). Politicians and the public prefer more argument, less figures. The multi-criteria analysis has the advantage that it can deal with various units of measurement, but its methodology is not so transparent nor so easy to communicate. The obtaining of weights can be quite a complex task of judgement, and is subjective rather than objective in some cases. Those who use a mixture of both cost-benefit analysis and the multi-criteria approach may still tend to focus on the monetary part of the process on the presumption that it appears more objective than the ratings methods.

There is therefore some merit in using matrices and check lists, which despite their limitations, are simple to construct and easy to understand, and can therefore encourage the use of a more integrated approach.

III.3. REFERENCES

1. ABBOTT P G, S M PHILLIPS, and R E LAYFIELD (1995). *Vehicle and traffic noise surveys alongside speed control cushions in York.* TRL Report 103, Transport Research Laboratory, Crowthorne.

2. ABBOTT, P G, S HARTLEY, A J HICKMAN, R.E.LAYFIELD, I.S.MCCRAE, P.M.NELSON, S M PHILLIPS, and J L WILSON (1995). *The Environmental Assessment of Traffic Management schemes, TRL Report 174.* Transport Research Laboratory, Crowthorne

3. DEPARTMENT OF TRANSPORT (1994). *Design manual for roads and bridges.* HMSO, London.

4. DEPARTMENT OF TRANSPORT (1995). *Valuation of Road accidents.* HMSO Department of Transport, London.

5. DEPARTMENT OF TRANSPORT (1988). *Calculation of road traffic noise.* HMSO, London

6. EUROPEAN UNION (1994). *Cost benefit and multi-criteria analysis for new road construction.* DOC EURET/385/94. European Commission, Brussels.

7. FINCH D, C R KOMPFNER, R LOCKWOOD and G MAYCOCK (1994). *Speed, speed limits and accidents.* TRL report PR58. Transport Research Laboratory, Crowthorne.

8. FRANKLIN R E, G HARLAND and P M NELSON (1979). *Road surfaces and traffic noise.* TRL Report LR896, Transport Research Laboratory, Crowthorne.

9. GRIFFITHS I D and G J RAW (1986*). Community and individual responses to changes in traffic noise exposure.* Journal of Sound and Vibration, 132(2), 331-336.

10. GRIMWOOD C J (1993). *A national survey of the effects of environmental noise on people at home.* Proceedings of the Institute of Acoustics, 15(8), 69-76.

11. LEVENTHALL H G (1987). *Low frequency traffic noise and vibration.* Transportation noise, Butterworth, London.

12. MINISTRY OF TRANSPORT OF DENMARK (1992). *The Danish Highway Investment Evaluation Model,* Road Directorate, Copenhagen.

13. OECD. Environment Directorate (1997). *Towards Sustainable Transportation,* Proceedings of the International Conference, organised by the OECD and hosted by the Government of Canada, Vancouver, British Columbia, 24-27 March 1996, OECD, Paris.

14. OECD. ROAD TRANSPORT RESEARCH (1994). *Environmental impact assessment of roads.* OECD, Paris.

15. OECD. Environment Directorate (1993). *Indicators for the integration of environmental concerns into transport policies.* Environment Monograph No 80. OECD, Paris.

16. RIKSREVISIONSVERKET (1988). *Vägverkets investeringsplanering.* Revisionsrapport Dnr1988:716, Stockholm.

17. SUMMERSGILL I and RE LAYFIELD (1996). *Non junction accidents on urban single-carriageway roads.* TRL Report 183, Transport Research Laboratory, Crowthorne.

18. WHO (1993). *The Environmental Health Criteria Document on Community Noise.* Report on task force meeting, Dusseldorf, 24-28 November 1992, EUR/ICP/RUD 163, 1141g. WHO, Geneva.

19. PAYNE J W, BETTMAN J R and E J JOHNSON (1993). *The Adaptive Decision-Maker.* Cambridge University Press.

20. VÄGVERKET (1996). *Miljörapport 95 (Environment report 95).* Swedish National Road Administration.

21. LEE-GOSSELIN M.E.H. (1989). *Voluntary and Mandatory Restraint on Car-Use in Canada: What would people give up?* Proceedings, PTRC Transport and Planning 17th Summer Annual Meeting, Brighton, UK.

22. EUROPEAN COMMUNITY. *COST 313 Socio-economic cost of road accident.* EUR 15464, European Community, Luxembourg.

23. OECD. ROAD TRANSPORT RESEARCH (1994). *Targeted Road Safety Programmes.* OECD, Paris.

24. OECD. ROAD TRANSPORT RESEARCH (1995). *Roadside Noise Abatement.* OECD, Paris.

CHAPTER IV   SYNTHESIS OF CURRENT PRACTICES

This Chapter presents the status of safety/environment integration based on responses to the questionnaire. Some additional efforts were made to obtain supplementary sources of information through research organisations in Member countries. Section IV.1 provides a brief portrait of how goals are expressed and how they are pursued through different organisational arrangements. This subject is too wide for the Group to have provided a complete catalogue of "best practice" from the material it received; but Section IV.2 is an exploration of the main types of integration possible. *The case examples presented were chosen because both safety and environmental issues are addressed*: this means that examples addressing only one of these issues were excluded, even if highly reputed. Section IV.3 is a synthesis of findings from the case material, augmented by some earlier findings on innovation in the urban transport context. The synthesis includes the identification of key ingredients for successful integrated strategies.

IV.1. DEFINITION OF GOALS AND ORGANISATIONAL RESPONSIBILITIES

Though the scope of environmental and traffic safety goals is very broad, those applied in practice in different countries show marked similarity. Many goals, for instance for air quality, are linked to international conventions while others, for instance for noise, have evolved through a more informal process. However, the ways in which goals are expressed or how their implementation is evaluated, show larger differences.

IV.1.1. *Themes*

One can generally say that the national level is by far the most important level in the definition of goals. Regional and local goals are often directly derived from the national goals. The national goals are in most countries based on laws, sometimes even set into laws themselves.

A relevant difference is that between, on the one hand, defining goals in overall results for the aspect observed, including the contributions from all the different sectors, such as traffic, industries, households, and, on the other hand, focusing on the consequences attributable to traffic alone, as absolute totals, as rates – for example with respect to the vehicle kilometres – or in terms of contributions per individual vehicle. Also, governments may express goals in terms of percentage changes in absolute totals, such as "a 25 per cent reduction in traffic fatalities by the year 2005" (indeed, in the case of human victims, it is rare to express a target such as "kill fewer than 1500 people"). Yet another possibility is to express the goals in terms of an intervening variable, such as the number of cold starts per year. The use of a specific kind of variable often already indicates whether one wants to influence the magnitude of mobility as whole, human behaviour, the technical functioning of the car, rural and urban planning, etc.

Goals for air quality are to a great extent influenced by international treaties, but there is a large diversity in the actual definition of the goals. Noise goals are expressed through accepted noise levels, but the consideration of exposure varies. Almost all countries have goals for traffic safety, and those that have goals express them in terms of reducing the total number of killed. In a number of cases the total number of injured is also of importance. The goals are set by or through the Ministry of Transport, sometimes after (or in) a parliamentary procedure.

IV.1.2   Implementation of goals

In the spread of responsibilities for implementing goals on traffic safety and environment one can see the complexity of the modern society. Apart from the Ministries for Transport and Environment, other ministries get involved, such as those responsible for infrastructure and for water. Administrations responsible for the national road network also get involved. These administrations are often semi-detached from the ministry, or in some cases they are privately, commercially run for a part of the national network (toll roads). The regional or local governments are often required to fulfil their part of the national goals.

Important to the implementation of goals is the way they are specified in laws, rules, etc. They can focus on the targets to be reached or on the planning processes to be followed. They can be binding for the government level at which they are enacted, and possibly also for other government levels.

In general the goals are selected, defined, and set on a national level. The implementation takes place for a large part within the lower administrations. Different forms of involvement of the national administration in the local or regional implementation can be seen: setting goals and limits that have to be observed, setting aside funds to finance projects that meet specific criteria, or developing tools and methods. This partly shows the priorities assigned to different aspects: some aspects are driving forces to start projects while others have to be reckoned with 'only' when a project is being developed.

IV.1.3.   Evaluation and integration of goals

The use of quantitative goals helps in putting a specific aspect into the evaluation and decision making process. It also leads to evaluation systems where, through these quantitative criteria, the advantages and disadvantages of different alternatives are made explicit. Of course this does not lead automatically to a choice that favours the environmental or traffic safety aspects. During the political decision making process weights are applied, and economic factors and the desirability of better infrastructure may decide. But it is in this process that the combination of traffic safety and environmental goals into one integrated strategy may be profitable for both, unless there is a conflict between the two fields. An identification of these fields or possible conflicts can therefore be of great use.

When qualitative goals are defined and translated into qualitative criteria, this still leaves the question of integrating all the criteria into an overall evaluation of a specific project. Although the answers on the questionnaire sometimes suggest otherwise, it appears that the problem of cost-benefit analysis, putting a value on non-material values, comes back in multi-criteria analysis in essentially the same form. The problem, for instance, of deciding how to weigh the difference in investment costs between two alternatives for a new road versus the number of people disturbed by its noise, seems almost to be the same as deciding on the monetary value of noise.

IV.1.4. *The decision process*

Decisions affecting environmental and safety aspects are being made at a wide variety of moments and in very different contexts.

It has already been observed that goals can be expressed in different ways: as totals for a country, absolutely or relative, or focused on the individual car. The decision context can thus be the definition or implementation of traffic or environmental policy in general at the national, regional or local level, on particular infrastructure or on regulations or norms governing the design of cars or roads. In all these instances it is important to have goals for both traffic safety and relevant environmental aspects in order to be able to combine them in such a way that it can be beneficial to both fields. Sometimes this will have to be goals focusing on the outcome for the surroundings, sometimes focusing on the performance of the different components of the traffic system.

The context wherein decisions are made deserves some attention. Sometimes this will be limited to an almost technical rundown of targets, criteria, a set of computational rules and exact calculations. But more often the societal context will play its role, either because public opinion has implicit influence on the decisions or because the decision is part of an explicit political process. The way different aspects are weighed in such a process is thus influenced by the forces present in the societal context where a specific decision is being made. The better these aspects are operationalised within the framework of an evaluation method, the more chance they have to take part in the implicit or explicit optimisation that then takes place.

IV.2. SELECTED CASE EXAMPLES

The objective of the case review was to reflect the nature and extent of the integration of safety and environmental considerations in contemporary road transport planning. A large number of examples could be found to illustrate the state of practice with respect to either safety or environmental issues taken alone, but these cases were excluded by definition from the review. The cases received from Member countries were extremely varied in nature, scope and geographical coverage. Even though the review was restricted to those in which both safety and environmental issues were addressed, it was not feasible to attempt a complete and representative catalogue of relevant initiatives within the OECD. Rather, the review sets out to identify the diversity of case experience using a classification scheme.

IV.2.1. *The classification scheme for cases*

From a preliminary review of the cases received, the Group observed that cases could best be classified using a matrix composed of two dimensions.

First dimension: decision contexts

The form and geographical extent of the cases could best be distinguished by the institutional context, but without regard to the degree of centralisation of government responsibility which differs substantially among Member countries. The first three categories on this dimension concern the management of road transport facilities, while the fourth is added to cover experience with safety and environmental regulation affecting vehicles and road users:

A. Major infrastructure – here, the decisions concern the assessment, building, evaluation and management of such major facilities as bridges, tunnels and motorways, typically under the control of national or state ministries but increasingly involving the private sector.

B. Corridor management – this includes decisions about corridors or networks of main roads, and recognises a growing interest in managing safety and environmental matters for ensembles of facilities along corridors between and within conurbations, often involving multiple jurisdictions.

C. Area transport and land-use planning – this decision context concerns the comprehensive management of transport within urban regions, most usually under the responsibility of metropolitan or inter-municipal government agencies.

D. State norms, regulations and economic policies for vehicles and road users – the geographical extent of relevant vehicle and road-user regulation is normally at the national or state level through manufacturing or use standards and inspection systems (safety, exhaust emissions), and through global traffic regulations such as overall speed limits.

A vast array of experience within either the safety or the environmental domains can be documented, thus the classes defined by combinations of the above categories may not be adequate for all such experience. However, the present objective is to organise case material where there is joint consideration of safety and environmental factors.

Second dimension: the "life-stage" of case experience

It is important to recognise that cases can consist of the establishment of policy and of evaluation methodology, "talking and planning", to use the stages identified in a Canadian report on urban travel and sustainable development (6), as well as examples of implemented practice, "acting and accomplishing". On this dimension, there are three categories, which can be seen as overlapping life-stages of case experience.

i) *Policy and plan development* – mostly laws or regulatory frameworks, either adopted or proposed, or statements of national, state or regional goals;

ii) *Evaluation frameworks* – the emphasis here is on evaluation or assessment methods which include criteria in both the safety and environmental domains;

iii) *Implemented projects/policies* – actual experience in Member countries of applying policies and evaluation frameworks.

Table IV.1. **Classification of cases**

	"LIFE STAGE" OF CASE EXPERIENCE		
DECISION CONTEXT	**(i)** Policy development	**(ii)** Evaluation frameworks	**(iii)** Implemented projects/policies
Major infrastructure	Norway, Sweden, Finland • Comparison of strategic roads policies Europe, North America • Private financing, e.g. DFBO policies (design, finance, build, operate)	France • Major road and multi-modal Great Britain • Trunk roads Denmark, Norway • Highway investment	Great Britain • Twyford Down motorway link
Corridor management	Canada • Quebec main highways with devolution	Netherlands • Amsterdam-Utrecht corridor Norway • Problem zones on main roads	Europe • Main roads crossing towns Europe, North America • Transport Telematics for Corridors
Area transport and land-use planning	Hungary • Action programme Norway • Transport planning 10 largest urban areas Finland • Transportation systems planning in urban regions Canada • Greater Toronto study France • 3 scenarios for Lyon Great Britain • Transport planning packages for local areas	Canada • BC highways social costing in Greater Vancouver	Denmark • Århus Canada • Urban cases Austria • Graz Temp 30/50 Switzerland • Zürich Europe, North America • Car-sharing associations Germany • Transport telematic for areas Austria • Eisenstadt
State norms, regulations and economic policies	United States • MVSS, CAFE and air quality	Finland • Winter roads	United States • 55 mph speed limit Europe, North America • Vehicle inspection and maintenance

59

While examples have been sought in each of the twelve cells defined by the four decision contexts and the three "life-stages" of case experience, individual examples sometimes encompass more than one type of case experience.

IV.2.2. *Cases about the construction of major infrastructure*

i) Policy and plan development

Norwegian, Swedish and Finnish strategic road plans

Since 1989, Norway has had a strategic road plan dealing with investments and maintenance of the national roads. It is presently being revised and will in 1997 be presented to the parliament. The new plan is based on four different alternatives; one putting emphasis on environmental aspects, one on safety, one on improved access to remote areas, and one putting emphasis on mobility. The plan will have a ten year perspective and the decision on profile will be taken by the parliament.

In 1995, Sweden made a special plan for environment and safety to complement the road plan, which is very similar to the Norwegian plan. Non-infrastructure measures are assembled in this environment and safety plan. Example targets are to lower the increase in traffic, to reduce speeding and to increase bicycle helmet usage, etc. In 1997, Sweden will produce a plan that consists of a road transport system plan integrating both infrastructure and non-infrastructure measures and will emphasise environmental and road safety goals.

In Finland, the National Road Safety Plan 1997-2000 defines five areas of emphasis:

- curbing growth in traffic,
- improving road safety in built-up areas,
- improving interaction between road users,
- reducing drunken driving,
- reducing running-off and head-on collision accidents and alleviating their consequences.

Links to environmental concerns are stressed in the context of the interaction of transport and land use. Growth in traffic is to be curbed by preventing the disintegration of the community structure. For built-up areas, the plan demands "safe, healthy, stimulating and comfortable living environments", noting that "an environment planned to cater for children, the elderly and the disabled offers safe travel opportunities for all" (1). Though the plan is mainly sectoral in character, the measures presented for influencing car mileage, community structure and land use have been defined to equal those that were included in the Transport Ministry Action Programme 1995-2000, published in 1994, to reduce the adverse effects of transport on the environment.

Private financing policies for major road infrastructure in Europe and North America

There has been a substantial increase in the private funding of such infrastructure as bridges, tunnels and motorways in recent years in a number of OECD countries. Examples of private investment include the second Severn Bridge in England, Highway 407 in Ontario, Canada, and the Los Angeles-San Bernadino tollway in California, USA. In France and Italy, inter-urban motorways are mostly operated by private sector concessions or quasi-private organisations. This trend is of interest here for two reasons.

First, policies such as Britain's "Design-Finance-Build-Operate" (DFBO) are conceived as ways to share the financial risk of major infrastructure developments between private and public sectors. Compared to conventional government procurement practices, this provides a novel climate for public debate about the choice of solutions in light of safety and environmental concerns, especially as such policies are promoted as efficient ways to generate design alternatives with reduced capital costs. However, the risks associated with delays in project construction and the costs of compensating those who are physically displaced remain, in general, the dominant issues.

Secondly, these policies generally provide for user charges to recover the cost of investments, reinforcing a trend for both publicly and privately financed projects. Charging policies are negotiated and, to varying extents, regulated by the central government. A key point is that the regulating agencies may be more concerned than the construction consortia with the recovery of the full social costs and the region-wide effects of different tolling policies.

Some general concerns with tolls were cited by several countries, notably Britain and Hungary. If tolls are high, some classes of traffic may be encouraged to divert to roads where there is a higher likelihood of accident and environmental impacts. If tolls are modest or eliminated, the new facility may induce traffic growth and land-use changes, the effects of which may overwhelm the benefits calculated for the new facility on the basis of historical demand trends. These issues are discussed in a 1993 British government discussion paper (2) and a 1994 report on the question of induced demand.

ii) Evaluation frameworks

The assessment of major roads and modal alternatives for interurban transport in France

The French questionnaire describes a planning and assessment process which is typical of a number of countries. The development of major new infrastructure is subjected to a multi-stage review process for environmental impacts. In the case of roads, this concerns wide study zones which include possible routes, narrowing progressively down to a 1 km, then 300m wide band as the project becomes more concrete. The safety benefits of alternative types of road are considered early in the process and are part of the justification for investment. Noise, air and water pollution, land-take, severance and other impacts are compared for specific alternatives and monitored for up to 10 years after construction. In the case of intermodal comparisons, 1995 directives from the Ministry of Transport provide values for safety and environment in cost-benefit analyses, but safety was initially absent from new assessment tools for intermodal choices developed by the Ministry of the Environment. Recently, however, monetary values for safety and environmental effects have been harmonised for rural situations and work is underway for such harmonisation in urban situations.

Trunk road assessment in Britain

The statutory procedures which apply to the approval of trunk road schemes in Britain involve numerous steps of technical analysis, publication of proposals, public consultation and, in the case of opposition, Public Inquiry. The approach is described in detail in the Department of Transport's "Design Manual for Roads and Bridges" (20), in which Volume 5 deals with the assessment and preparation of road schemes. The major evaluation framework is the COBA (cost-benefit analysis) which places major emphasis on the value of time savings and of reductions in accidents predicted for new roads. But the procedure also requires that environmental consequences are taken into account by preparing an Environmental Assessment in the form of an Environmental Impact Table, which goes alongside the engineering, traffic forecasting and economic assessment of the proposed scheme compared with a do minimum option.

Highway investments in Denmark and Norway

Many other countries use cost-benefit models to decide on highway investments. One example is Denmark where the road directorate has developed a PC based model. The model includes economic estimates of travel time, vehicle operating costs, accidents, noise and air pollution, barrier effects and risk perception, operation and maintenance costs as well as construction and rehabilitation costs. Similar models are in use in the other Nordic countries as a means for making an input into the planning process. A Canadian example is the BC Highways social costing model which has been tested in the Vancouver urban region.

The Norwegian impact assessment handbook (4) deals with the co-ordinated assessment and presentation of traffic flow, safety, environment, natural resources, land use structure and scheme costs. Quantifiable and non-quantifiable impacts are dealt with separately, but they are part of a unified framework. Calculated cost/benefit rates are related to qualitatively assessed impacts according to the following guideline: "The alternatives are systematically compared to resolve whether they are better than the do-nothing alternative, and how they relate to each other".

The criterion as to whether an alternative is profitable, compared to the do-nothing alternative, is that its net rate of return is positive. If the rate is negative, there must be considerable qualitative benefits to characterise this alternative as "better than" the do-nothing alternative. On the other hand, if the rate of return is positive, the qualitatively assessed impacts must be strongly negative to characterise this alternative as "worse than" the do-nothing alternative (4). Traffic safety is assessed through accident costs. For environmental impacts, a monetary value is given for barrier effects. Other environmental impacts are qualitatively assessed using a 9-point scale.

iii) Implemented projects/policies

Britain: Twyford Down motorway link

After what some environmental groups saw as a "watershed" public debate about the encroachment of major road infrastructure on the rural landscape, in 1992 the UK government approved the completion of a missing portion of a major motorway route between London and Southampton through an upland area known as Twyford Down. This was an example of a major conflict between environmental benefits, notably aesthetic and wildlife considerations, and predicted accident reduction, as the road replaced was both overloaded and hazardous. The debate was particularly acrimonious and continued when some environmental activists attempted to block construction by physical action.

One result of the debate was a recommendation by experts to move the assessment of environmental acceptability to the very early stages of infrastructure project planning, and this is now reflected in official documents (3). It was hoped that this recommendation would make the search for the least damaging alternatives more efficient and, in some respects, pre-empt recent EU requirements for environmental impact assessment in such cases. Nevertheless, major road development projects have continued to attract conspicuous protest, and some approved projects have been the target of highly publicised actions by protesters who have occupied trees, tunnels or buildings in the path of new construction. Some protests may go beyond the local impacts of road schemes, and may be seen as symbolic battles over central government policy on increased motorisation. Similar protests over land-take, loss of trees or other environmental impacts have occurred in France and the Netherlands.

IV.2.3. **Corridor management cases**

Corridors are almost by definition a source of challenge to institutional and political boundaries, especially if they form part of a national road network. Even though a single government department may have responsibility for the road, the adjoining land use and local road network are usually governed by local agencies.

i) Policy and plan development

Canada : Quebec corridor management of devolved provincial highways

Under Canada's federal system, road infrastructure is entirely within provincial government jurisdiction and provinces differ in the degree to which the road system is managed. In Quebec, a very recent development is the devolution of responsibility for about one third of the primary road network to regional and urban municipalities. This has been accompanied by an increased demand from the municipalities for technical assistance from the provincial transport ministry at a time when the ministry's workforce is being reduced.

One major response is the current development of management tools for the integrated treatment of corridors. The policy provides for a reduced level of personnel in regional bureaux but to develop enhanced technical assistance on a province-wide basis, such as expert systems to identify abnormally high accident locations and suitable solutions. Increasingly, "integrated diagnosis" methods for unsafety (notably hazards to pedestrians and cyclists), noise, visual intrusion, degradation of historic buildings and neighbourhoods, barrier effects, migration of economic activities and land-use conflicts are being brought into the corridor management procedure, but not as yet within a single evaluation framework. In North America, corridors often include traditional "main streets" in the urban areas they traverse, and these have been the target of a number of social and economic revitalisation programmes (in Quebec, the programme "Rues principales" of Heritage Canada) which are coherent with the integrated diagnosis approach.

ii) Evaluation frameworks

Netherlands: Corridor Amsterdam-Utrecht (CAU)

The CAU study project concerns the corridor between Amsterdam and Utrecht, the first and fourth cities by size of the Netherlands. The two cities are about twenty kilometres apart and are linked by a motorway, a railroad and a major class waterway, the Amsterdam–Rhine canal, all running almost side by side. Both the motorway and the railroad are at capacity during large periods of the day. On the Utrecht side, a large new town is being developed across the road (30 000 houses).

In an integrated study different combinations of actions are considered for the transport of people and goods. The effects on overall congestion, safety, living circumstances and barrier effects are considered, together with overall costs. The different actions include enlargement of the road, new road construction, road pricing, or enclosing some or all of the road network. A combination of actions evolves as optimal, consisting of enlargement of both road and rail, as well as enclosing essential parts of the road to strengthen the link between Utrecht and the new town.

Problem zones on Norwegian main roads

In Norway, a method has been developed that allows for assessment of the environmental and safety situation in the existing road network. The method describes problem zones with respect to noise, air pollution, landscape characteristics and traffic safety. This is integrated into an overall assessment that is put into the road data base. The system was set up in 1991 with data collection since then and a demonstration project will probably start in 1998.

iii) Implemented projects/policies

Treatment of main roads crossing small European towns and villages

A number of programmes have focused on the problems of main roads crossing small towns and villages, implementing design modifications to the road and its immediate surroundings, signing, and parking regulations. Typically, the primary objective is speed and accident reduction but also the mitigation of environmental problems such as noise and severance for residents. A review of approaches adopted in Denmark, Belgium, France, and Germany will be found in (5), and a detailed explanation of a French methodology in (15).

Aneby, in Sweden, is a recent example in which both safety and environmental issues were prominent. Aneby is a small town in the southern part of Sweden. A national road passes through the town and has been creating both safety problems, which were mainly for pedestrians and bicyclists, and environmental problems, which consisted of noise and air pollution and barrier effects. In 1994, the local municipality and the national road administration jointly decided to do something about these problems and in 1995 the redesigned road was opened.

The process leading to the opening of the redesigned road includes a great deal of involvement on behalf of the citizens of the municipality. The preliminary plans were presented including a description of safety and environmental problems along the road, and different target groups were invited to participate in the design of the project. The target groups included local shop owners, inhabitants near the road, schools and others. The result of this process was twofold, first the redesign was in many aspects a very radical one, and second there were no complaints from the general public due to the large amount of participation. A somewhat similar approach has been taken to mitigate the effects of traffic transiting Ampuis, France, a small town south of Lyon on the N86, one of the three major north-south roads in the Rhône corridor.

In Denmark, the main through roads of three towns, Vinderup, Skaerbaek and Ugerlose, underwent experimental treatments of this kind and the results on traffic safety and the environment were generally positive (16). However, in Britain, recent studies of traffic calming on main roads in villages such as Thorney, Cambridgeshire and Craven Arms, Shropshire, have found public reaction to be generally unfavourable even though traffic was slowed (17, 18). This was attributed partly to public preferences for proposals to build by-passes, and partly to residents' perceptions of increased noise and vibration in association with some calming devices, in spite of the fact that most objective measures of noise and vibration showed improvements. Reactions to changes in the localisation and type of noise and vibration thus seem to have more than offset the benefits which residents identified from lower traffic speeds.

The layout of the urban road through Rantasalmi, a small Finnish town, was revised in 1993. The road was narrowed to 6.5 meters throughout and to 5.5 meters at pedestrian and cycle crossings.

A speed limit of 40 km/h was set for the central area. Other traffic calming measures such as raised sections of carriageways were used at certain locations. The evaluation showed among other things:

- lower speeds
- speeds of heavy vehicles lowered more than speed of light vehicles
- lower noise levels
- amount of traffic down, especially heavy vehicles
- no effect on fuel consumption
- maintenance costs increased
- both drivers and residents were pleased with the redesign of the road

Generally, this seems to be a typical example of the effects to expect when applying traffic calming measures.

Europe/North America: Transport Telematics for Corridors

One of the programmes in the third European Union Framework-programme of DRIVE is the STIG programme (Systèmes Télématiques d'Intérêt Général). The work in this programme builds on the exploratory research in the DRIVE programme from the 2nd Framework-programme. The aim is to improve performance (both safety and efficiency) of the trans-European traffic system, while reducing impact of transport on the environment. Some of the corridor projects which are of interest in the context of this group's work are described here, while some area projects are described in IV.2.4. Most of these projects are at the pilot stage of implementation.

An example of a corridor managemnet project is the PLEIADES project, focusing on the Paris-London corridor. The goal is to combine the activities in the field of travel and traffic information with those in inter-urban traffic management, resulting in a demonstration of an integrated driver information and network management system in the corridor. Among the participants are car companies, government bodies, broadcasting companies, research institutions and the Eurotunnel company.

A similar corridor management project is MELYSSA (Mediterranean-Lyon-Stuttgart Site for ATT). It is planned to significantly improve road transport efficiency, safety and environment by enhancing traffic information and its provision to all road users. Attention is paid primarily to the motorway and possibly to the railway corridor.

Similar projects are also either operational or under development in North America, such the COMPASS project in the Toronto area, for which major energy, pollution and accident-reduction benefits have been claimed (8).

IV.2.4. *Area transport and land-use planning cases*

i) **Policy and plan development**

Hungarian transport policy and action programme

In a decision made in 1996, the Hungarian parliament set out the strategy for "The Hungarian transport policy and the most important tasks in its implementation". Among other things, the transportation system should:

- result in improving road safety;
- meet requirements for environmental protection;
- satisfy the conditions of sustainable development.

The Hungarian Government will produce an Action Programme by 1997 for the implementation of eleven decisions taken in the context of this policy. Some of the decisions concern supporting combined goods transport and public transport, limiting passenger car traffic in densely populated regions and historical regions, and establishing the conditions for safe pedestrian and bicycle traffic.

Norway: Transport Planning for the ten largest urban areas (TP 10)

In 1989, a project was started in Norway to promote new methods for transport planning. The focus was on concerns related to increasing environmental problems, capacity problems and rising costs for traffic in urban areas. The emphasis was on co-operation among local authorities, with central authorities giving technical support and developing guidelines. No explicit emphasis was mentioned on safety issues. Transport planning in the ten urban areas was meant to introduce new thinking compared to earlier road and transport plans with respect to the following:

- co-ordination of land use and transport policies;
- co-ordination of all public investments and management;
- give priority to public transport as a tool for environmental policy;
- clarification of measures to reduce the increase in car traffic;
- development of scenarios for alternative transportation systems with a varying degree of private and public transport;
- consideration of different measures within a joint budget framework.

The evaluation shows that the initiative indeed led to a considerable work and collaboration between different local parties. However, the results show a traditional approach to road planning with little concern for land use issues or other alternative ways of solving environmental problems. The county road departments and the municipal departments of town planning dominated the process, whereas the county departments for communication and transport or environment played lesser roles. The conclusion is that the need for organisational changes or stronger guidelines was underestimated by the central authorities. According to the evaluation report (19), the intention that integrated planning in TP 10 should contribute to a marked change in course in environmental politics seemed to have failed.

Finland: Transportation System Planning (TSP) in urban regions

Finland has developed a concept of TSP in Urban Regions, which by the year 2000 is expected to extend to the 20 urban regions with more than 50 000 inhabitants in the country. The concept was produced through close co-operation between the Ministry of Transport and Communications, the Ministry of the Environment, the Association of Finnish local authorities, the Finnish National Road Administration, and the Finnish State Railways. The emphasis is put on:

- co-operation between different organisations,
- simultaneous planning of different transport modes,
- integration of land use and transportation planning,
- environmental aspects,
- better level of service in public transport,

- improvements for pedestrians and bicyclists,
- cost-efficient approach.

Goals are set for sustainability, safety, transport mode co-operation, road and street network, goods transport, transport management and financing. The major benefits sought are the simultaneous planning of different modes of transport and the possibility to reduce the need for infrastructure construction with the aid of transport system management. A 1997 evaluation of 9 transport system plan processes found a clear improvement in defining and implementing transport policy, especially in regard of transport mode co-operation and the service level and safety for pedestrians and bicyclists. But the links to urban structure, location of activities and land use planning were only slightly improved. There were difficulties in dealing with goods transport.

Canada: Office of Greater Toronto Area Study

A 1992 study (9) of the state of the environment in the watershed area corresponding to the greater region of Toronto evoked sufficient public and political interest that it was enlarged into a comprehensive review of urban development and land use policy for the region. Eventually, three scenarios were elaborated, each with a strong transport component: a laissez faire policy towards further expansion of low-density settlement in surrounding agricultural areas, the re-concentration of growth within the existing urban core, and the increase in settlement density around satellite centres with high levels of transit service between centres and to the centre of Toronto. While not focused on accident reduction as such, a significant element of the policy debate was on the degree of car-dependence implied and especially upon the calculation, by the Ontario Ministry of Transportation, that there were unlikely to be sufficient public funds available to pay for the highway network required by any of the three scenarios under conventional assumptions of vehicle trip generation.

France: Three scenarios for a debate on the future of urban travel in Lyon

The authorities of the greater Lyon region presented to the public, in September 1996, three alternatives packages of planning principles which could be adopted to guide urban transport development. The three scenarios differed in the relative importance of infrastructure and regulation in support of private cars, non-motorised transport and public transport. In an exhibition and a report, an image of the next 10 years was given together with a qualitative evaluation of each in terms of the consequences for noise, air quality, quality of urban space, congestion and, in a very general way, accidents. Equity of access, public costs and likely public support was also discussed. The public was asked to express their preference for one of the scenarios and nine working groups were charged with elaborating recommendations on the planning principles to be adopted.

Great Britain: Packages of local authority transport planning measures

In Britain, the central government has recently added two policy instruments to encourage municipalities and counties to reduce the need for private car travel through complementary sets of interventions. First, the Department of Transport and the Department of the Environment jointly issued Planning Policy Guidelines on Transport (PPG13) that cover the siting of traffic generating activities and a number of road, parking and public transport development issues. The Department of the Environment also issued PPG6 on retailing and town centres.

Secondly, since 1993, central government aid to local authorities for transport projects is partly dependent upon a system of Transport Policies and Programme (TPP) submissions, in which integrated packages of measures bid for funding against criteria and priorities announced on an annual basis (12). While encouraging the use of conventional quantitative criteria such as projected reductions in accidents or motor vehicle travel time, it was envisaged that guidance would gradually be provided on the use of a wider set of criteria, based on accumulated experience with the TPP system. These instruments have explicitly required the simultaneous consideration of safety and environmental objectives, but they have also heightened awareness, by both central and local governments, of the difficulty of assigning values to widely diverse impacts.

One of the first successful TPP bidders, the County of Oxfordshire, in submitting a package affecting the historic core of the city of Oxford, chose to attempt an economic justification of some environmental benefits that are not quantified in the conventional UK cost-benefit framework. Some effort was also made to quantify other benefits such as reductions in delays to pedestrians and cyclists, and economic vitality through increased tourism. The methodology used for the successful bid was welcomed by the Department of Transport in its response, although it described some of the evaluations of Package benefits as "unconventional" (13). It is pointed out by the same reference that the first round (1994) of supplementary guidance to those preparing TPPs gave a "guarded" reception to the use of monetary values for a wide set of environmental impacts, and to the inclusion of economic vitality benefits in the evaluation of a Package.

More recently, in the City of York's 1997/98 bid, each element of the package is assessed qualitatively, compared to a "do minimum" condition, on a four point scale (negative, neutral, positive, very positive) for a variety of traffic indicators, including accidents, and for several environmental and economic impact indicators touching different user groups.

ii) Evaluation frameworks

Canada: BC Highways social costing in Greater Vancouver

The British Columbia Department of Highways has developed an integrated social costing methodology. This is of particular interest in the rapidly urbanising areas of Greater Vancouver, where there is pressure for road building in spite of the region's reputation as the most "anti-motorway" conurbation in Canada. In principle, the evaluation method provides the elements for an informed public debate about competing investments in private versus public transport, but in practice its outputs are often not visible in particular cases. "According to comments received from the chairman of the regional Council of mayors, this is partly explained by ambiguity in the respective roles of the provincial and regional government institutions in setting development priorities, which means it is very difficult for safety and environmental considerations to be given a level playing field. The result is that the political debate often focuses on relieving congestion with little regard to the consequences either for accidents or environmental quality".

iii) Implemented projects/policies

Denmark : Århus

The Danish municipality of Århus presented in 1993 what was called a planning theme for transport and environmental quality. The project covers problem description, targets and priority areas of action for six different aspects: energy consumption, air pollution, noise, road safety, barrier effects and the visual environment. Each of the six priority areas of action is discussed under four headings: planning, public works and purchasing, traffic management and information and education. It is a very comprehensive project attempting to take a quality perspective of road transport.

However, the scheme is goal oriented and little effort is made to describe the strategies for reaching these goals.

Canada: Initiatives toward more sustainable urban travel

A 1993 review of the status of sustainable transportation in major Canadian cities (6) rated 25 types of initiatives under seven headings:

- urban structure/design policies,
- transportation infrastructure,
- demand management practices,
- transit management practices,
- traffic management practices,
- cleaner vehicle technology development,
- public outreach and awareness programmes.

The review rated the status of each type of initiative as having reached "talking, planning, acting or accomplishing", in a significant portion of major cities, as well as in one or two cities with more advanced implementations. Although the study did not consider negative cross-impacts between environment and safety, it is interesting to note which of the initiatives were judged by the authors to have a large impact on "greater safety", as well as positive impacts on environmental sustainability. Seven were so judged: compact mixed land-use; pedestrian-friendly streets; congestion pricing for road use; high-occupancy vehicle facilities; rapid transit and commuter rail networks; cycle and pedestrian ways; fare integration and schedule co-ordination; and traffic calming. Only one of these – rapid transit and commuter rail networks was among the six types of initiative which have reached the "acting" stage in a significant portion of major cities.

However, two out of four types of initiative that have reached the "acting" stage in *no* major Canadian cities were in the safety impact list: compact mixed land-use, and congestion pricing for road use.

Tempo 30/50 in Graz, Austria

In 1980 the first streets of Graz were designated as "Tempo 30" streets: a speed limit of 30 km/h, clear physical indications at the entrances, changes on cross-section of the street, and in this case combine with "alternating parking". A few years later two city parts were designed as Tempo-30 zones. The public acceptance of these measures was such that more than 80 parts of the city requested to be designated as Tempo-30 zone. This would mean a major investment, a twenty- or thirty-year rebuilding programme and a flood of traffic signs. Therefore another course was followed: the whole of the city was designated as Tempo-30 zone through signs and messages on the entrance roads to the city. A speed of 50 km/h was allowed only on designated right-of-way streets. A research programme to detect changes before and after was started, focusing on speeds at selected points and on routes, route choice, noise, exhaust fumes, accidents, traffic behaviour, acceptance by drivers and population (10).

Traffic safety showed a major improvement. The primary cause of this was considered to be growing awareness through the discussions and the publicity campaigns, given that marked differences in traffic behaviour were observed. Car-drivers paid more attention to pedestrians, and made fewer overtaking manoeuvres with respect to bicycles; pedestrians and bicyclists behaved more confidently. The diminished speed level contributed also, although the mean speed level went down less than expected and hoped for (e.g. from 25.2 km/h to 23.0 km/h at mid-block). The deviation however was also smaller, so the traffic flow became more homogeneous. It was concluded that the reduction of speed should be improved through intensification of the publicity campaign and police control.

The noise level went down to a barely detectable level, caused by the lower speeds. There was little change in exhaust emission levels for the city as a whole. However, within the Tempo-30 streets the NO_x emissions decreased significantly.

Publicity campaigns and police control were essential parts of the model as applied in Graz, and it was considered that this should continue permanently. The acceptance by car-drivers improved continuously. The general evaluation by the researchers was positive, and they suggest that the model not be considered as a single measure, but rather as an essential part of the general concept for traffic development in the city.

Switzerland: "less traffic – more Bern"

Under the title "Less traffic – more Bern" the mayor of Bern confronted the citizens in 1983 with the impossibility of accommodating the growing demand for space by traffic while keeping the 800-year-old city centre, a UNESCO World Heritage site, intact.

It was recognised that one cannot continue to provide total freedom for individuals in the choice of mode and time of transport. This was the main drive behind the programme that was consequently developed. Other environmental aspects and traffic safety were not an explicit factor at that time, but safety for pedestrian, bicyclist and public transport users came to be a necessary factor in the programme. The main points of the programme were the following:

- Promotion of public transport by heavy investments and a strict priority in the traffic system, especially in the centre,

- Channelling motorised through traffic into a basic network; therefore some essential bypasses were provided,

- Traffic calming measures in residential areas, reducing traffic, and making traffic through the centre impossible,

- New park-and-ride facilities in the periphery, strict control of inner city parking.

Switzerland: The Zurich conurbation transport policy

Zurich has followed a strategy of promotion of public transport for more than twenty years. This has been translated into giving priority to existing trams and buses, thus increasing speed and reliability. For that reason an extensive investment programme in computer technology has been executed, that gives almost complete control over the entire public transport system. A metro scheme on a regional scale has also been introduced. Nevertheless it proved necessary to actively and selectively reduce the attractiveness of the car as a possible choice for travel to and into the town in order to arrive at the goals set.

Therefore, in any conflict involving the various interests in the transport sector, precedence is given to public transport. Also, the capacity of the road network is restrained by converting car lanes into cycle or tram tracks. Other measures included shortening of green light times for car traffic, banning night driving on motorway access roads through residential areas, and parking space planning.

Car-sharing associations in Europe and North America

As an alternative to car ownership, or to multiple car ownership, car-sharing associations have grown substantially in Germany, Switzerland, the Netherlands and Austria since the late 1980s, and since 1991 a network of associations known as "European Car Sharing" allows over 20,000 members in 40 associations to receive reciprocal services in 250 towns. In Canada, a first association was launched in Quebec City in 1994, followed by Montreal a year later. They permit novel strategies for the organisation of personal travel which modify individuals' contributions to the generation of pollution and greenhouse gases and their exposure to accident risk.

Germany: Transport telematics for areas

Some telematics projects target the safety and environmental performance of road traffic on a region-wide basis (see IV.2.3 for projects focusing on corridors). As with the corridor examples, most of these projects are at the pilot stage of implementation.

The HERMES (High Efficiency Roads with Rerouting Methods and Traffic Signal Control) project tries to improve traffic safety and efficiency through improved knowledge of the current state of traffic in a given network, and the application of control strategies based on this knowledge. The main contribution is expected to be improved traffic flow and reduced congestion. Incident Detection will help to avoid secondary accidents. One of the test sites for the project will be another project: RHAPIT (Rhein-Main Area Project for Integrated Traffic), focuses on the interurban traffic in the Rhein-Main area, an area with one of the densest motorway networks in Europe. Infrastructure for traffic management (loop detectors, transmitters, signs, radio broadcast facilities) is already available on some roads.

Another example of an area-wide application is the planned regional traffic management system "STORM" for Stuttgart. This is intended to provide assistance when selecting the means of transport, the time to start the journey, the route and travelling behaviour, in order to increase safety and economy to adapt the traffic situation better to the environment. Six pilot projects are under way to test the measures needed in practice. The traffic information pilot project provides the users with data on suggested routes and times required, individual timetables for public transport and the comparison of costs. The inclusion of ticket purchase and parking space reservation possibilities is planned. The individual route guidance system for cars takes the current traffic situation into consideration, informs about car parks with vacancies and recommends switching to public transport as appropriate. Variable traffic signs indicate traffic jams and the parking situation. The connection information system transmits information on actual departure times to train platforms and regulates feeder bus departure timing.

Austria: Eisenstadt

During the period 1987 to 1995, a package of measures was introduced to address increasing car dependency in Eisenstadt, a relatively low-density settlement of about 10,000 inhabitants in eastern Austria. The package included a subsidised, flat-rate "City Taxi" service, the pedestrianisation of the entire city centre, improvements in bicycle infrastructure, traffic calming, parking measures – the elimination of central-area on-street parking coupled with new off-street, short-stay central parking and some free parking on the city edge – and motorway bypasses. In addition, land-use policies were

71

adopted to encourage business and industrial development outside the city centre. It has been claimed that the collective effect of these measures was to "break the strong growth of private car use despite the high and still growing rate of motorisation". This case appears to show that, even though the modal shift was small in percentage terms, concerted packages of measures can influence where and when private cars are used.

IV.2.5. *Nation- or state-wide regulation of vehicles and drivers*

i)   Policy and plan development

USA: Motor Vehicle Safety Standards, CAFE rules and Air Quality norms

Under the US federal system, public and private sectors alike are subjected to a variety of federal mandatory performance targets which may be met in flexible ways. This is applied to motor vehicle crashworthiness, fuel consumption and exhaust emissions. It is also applied to the air quality of metropolitan regions. There are state-level vehicle performance mandates in California and some other states, notably concerning emission standards and the introduction of low- or zero-emission vehicles.

All of these examples involve potential complementarities and some conflicts between safety and environmental targets. For example, Corporate Average Fuel Efficiency (CAFE) rules, whereby an automobile manufacturer must ensure that the sales-weighted average energy intensity of all new vehicles sold falls below a legal threshold, have encouraged the sale of smaller and lighter vehicles. A contentious argument has ensued over whether this must lead to increased accident trauma, and if so, what remedies are of greatest overall benefit to society. These mandatory performance targets are subject to intense lobbying and are not always sustained, but they have incited considerable technological creativity.

ii)   Evaluation frameworks

Finland: Winter Roads

In Finland a "road traffic in winter" research programme has been conducted to search for an optimal maintenance policy. The original situation can be described as one with high usage of studded tyres (> 95 per cent of passenger cars with studs) and a relatively high usage of salt (120 000 t/a). This was compared with different scenarios reducing both the usage of studs in tyres and salt usage. The costs associated with these different stud/salt alternatives was made up by accident costs, environmental costs (e.g. pollution of groundwater, vegetation damage, dust), maintenance costs and vehicle costs. As the research programme originated in a heated debate on de-icing salt use impacts on groundwater quality, a main target was seeking means to reduce the risks of salt use. The evaluation of the scenarios showed that human injury accident costs determine the choice of policy. Both a ban on stud use and ending de-icing salt use would lead to unacceptable accident risk and cost increases.

The new policy, adopted in 1995, emphasises targeted salt use, precision forecasting and new salt spreading techniques, halving annual salt consumption from the original level. The remaining groundwater quality risks are mitigated through protective structures.

iii) Implemented projects/policies

USA: 55 mph national speed limit

Implemented as a fuel-saving measure after the 1974 oil embargo, the national 55 mph speed limit has generally been credited with a reduction in road accident trauma. The debate since 1987, when the limit on rural motorways could be raised to 65 mph and more recently when federally mandated speed limits were removed, has taken on recent importance because of greenhouse gas emissions, which are closely related to fuel consumption. Road safety is widely believed to have deteriorated, but statistical indicators are sometimes criticised for taking insufficient account of the effects on alternative routes from which traffic may be diverted, or of the accompanying redeployment of traffic enforcement resources.

Europe and North America: Inspection and maintenance systems for private vehicles

Periodic Motor Vehicle Inspection for safe operating condition is implemented in many countries, but was largely abandoned in the 1970s in the USA after insufficient economic benefit could be demonstrated. More recently, inspection for pollution control has been increasingly added and inspection is seen as a complementary strategy with both safety and environmental benefits.

IV.3. SYNTHESIS

A number of inferences can be drawn from the evidence presented to the group in the questionnaires and case material.

First, in rather few cases is there a conscious effort to treat safety and environmental objectives within an integrated framework. Indeed, a distinction must be made between the co-ordination and the integration of safety and environmental questions. The former means that there is simultaneous consideration of the two, usually employing different methodologies, and is much easier to find. The latter implies that a trade-off between the two is made explicit to some degree, although not necessarily within a quantified framework.

Secondly, not only is co-ordination much more common than integration; co-ordination is also, in general, less influential and less transparent. However, where either occurs, it can be said that the outcome is typically positive in the sense that the decisions taken are perceived to be closer to the interests of the whole community than the alternatives which might otherwise have prevailed.

Thirdly, a recurrent theme is that the evaluation of multiple payoffs *must involve looking beyond the immediate boundaries of the scheme or project* – the whole neighbourhood around a traffic calming scheme, the whole main road network when tolling or a when a new speed limit is introduced on a motorway, etc. The evaluation methods which work best encourage decision-makers to weigh this wider evidence. The imperative to defend the fairness of a decision when only some of criteria used are quantifiable often leads to simplifications: qualitative and/or subjective evidence may be ignored unless it is persuasive enough to drive a veto.

Fourthly, there is much room *for innovation and experimentation* in interventions, particularly in evaluation frameworks and planning processes. Currently, interurban road transport, notably through corridor management, seems rather more amenable to innovation in planning processes than does urban transport. This may be because it has become normal to involve both transport and environmental agencies and interests in planning interurban transport.

Fifthly, some factors which contribute to the success of integrated road transport *planning processes* for safety and the environment can be inferred, as listed below. However, the intention is not to cover every stage of the planning process but to identify, from the questionnaires and cases, some key attributes of success:

1. Ask leading questions about safety and environmental goals at the conceptual stage of interventions.

2. Choose a level of public involvement which is appropriate to the scale and timing of the problems.

3. Detect instabilities – effects which will become political icons, symbolic fights, etc. – to avoid or to use. (Citizen rights vs. road-user duties).

4. Allow for logical paradoxes in what people will accept. (I cannot accept being killed but a certain number will be....also the asymmetry in measures of willingness to pay versus willingness to accept).

5. Give due consideration to "points of no return" (e.g., degree of neighbourhood separation, levels of public transport service, car ownership levels...).

6. Articulate possible comprehensive "packages" of transport system qualities (with estimated performance in safety and environmental terms, including projections over 5, 10, 15 ....years).

7. Recognise who (or which locality) wins and who loses as a result of a particular decision.

8. Make it possible to learn from past failures as well as successes.

Sixthly, some inferences can be drawn concerning the interventions which best serve safety and environmental goals, although it would be incorrect to suggest that there is, at this time, a consensus on "best practice". Urban area transport and land use planning cases dominate the case material that provides the greatest detail on interventions. In part, this is a consequence of the group's selection, but it also points to the importance of active regional and local administrations. This aspect is reinforced by earlier findings on the urban context reviewed in the ECMT/OECD report on urban travel (14).

Strategies for specific areas are both easier to assess and easier to implement than, for instance, general goals for travel demand reduction, and a growing number of administrations have undertaken ambitious urban redevelopment schemes. There is, on the other hand, little evidence that these actions successfully influence the trends in overall traffic growth or mode distribution in the wider regions to which they belong.

Innovative practices in land use management focused on limiting the spread of cities to keep up residential densities and protect open land, and increasing the supply of inner-city housing. Activities notably influencing the transport system, such as offices and shopping, were steered to city centres or other locations well served by public transportation, and freight distribution centres located close to existing main transport networks. Parking provision regulation took the form of low maxima on the number of car parking spaces provided at new office developments and parking supply was shifted from central and inner districts to park-and-ride interchanges.

Land use innovations included promotion of mixed uses or urban villages, establishment of car-free areas and measures to encourage development around existing public transport routes.

A basic means of road traffic management was regulating infrastructure provision: road investment directed to bypasses of sensitive areas, combined with traffic calming measures and other improvements in the areas bypassed. Extending pedestrian precincts and improving other bicycle and pedestrian facilities supported non-motorised traffic; reserved lanes, priorities for trams and buses, real-time information about services at all stops and about park-and-ride facilities supported public transport. Reducing speed limits to 30 km/h or lower in residential streets and other areas improved especially the safety of pedestrians and bicyclists.

Telematics could be used to integrate urban transport management, minimise congestion, improve air quality, facilitate pedestrian movement and provide real time information services for travellers. Large employers' commuter plans served to reduce the number of cars in use during the day. Promoting the use of low pollution buses and freight vehicles through environmental zoning, designating specified freight transport routes and limiting freight movement in sensitive areas at night served to protect the local environment.

Locally, traditional pricing policy concerned parking fees, to balance demand and supply for road use. Toll rings could finance infrastructure redevelopment. Businesses benefiting from improvements to transport could contribute towards the costs of those improvements. Electronic congestion pricing for inner cities and other areas could serve to at least reduce congestion, improving also the position of public transport. Additional local taxes could be used in more innovative ways than national fuel taxes. Local income from charging for road space and parking could be used to fund public transport and environmental improvements.

Pedestrianisation, improving public transport fares and service levels were seen as effective ways to improve traffic safety.

In the referred study, most cities listed the reduction of congestion or the management of transport demand as objectives, and many already had or were developing more comprehensive traffic plans or integrated transport strategies.

Finally, in this last respect, the urban area cases resemble the other types of case experience: it is possible to target a balance of environmental and road safety outcomes and, to varying degrees, demonstrate that they have been achieved. But integrated planning and evaluation works best in interventions of limited scale and/or complexity. From the experience of member countries, it appears unreasonable to expect or to seek the creation of new national institutions devoted solely to the integration or co-ordination of safety and environmental goals. If anything, the major institutional trend is towards decentralisation and deregulation, although some new regulatory structures emerging from that trend could well *incorporate* safety and environmental goals into their mandates.

In the light of these realities, the fact that the lessons learnt from successful integrated and co-ordinated environment/road safety strategies come from a wide variety of institutional settings should be seen as an advantage. Above all, they suggest that it is feasible to make environmental and unsafety consequences more explicit in most technical and public assessments of proposed changes to transport and land use. This would seem to be a prerequisite for realistic debate among and between affected parties and interested institutions. In the following chapter, we trace the history of institutional barriers and opportunities, and look briefly at how they may evolve in the future.

IV.4. REFERENCES

1. FINNISH MINISTRY OF TRANSPORT AND COMMUNICATIONS (1996). *Liikenneturvallisuussuunnitelma 1997-2000 (National Road Safety Plan 1997-2000)*. Publications 33/96. Helsinki.

2. DEPARTMENT OF TRANSPORT; SCOTTISH OFFICE; WELSH OFFICE (1993). *Paying For Better Motorways: Issues for Discussion*. Command Paper. 1993/05. (CM 2200) HMSO, London.

3. DEPARTMENT OF TRANSPORT STANDING ADVISORY COMMITTEE ON TRUNK ROAD ASSESSMENT (1994). *Trunk Roads and the Generation of Traffic*. HMSO, London.

4. STATENS VEGVESEN (1995). *Håndbok-140, konsekvensanalyser (Impact Assessment)*. Norwegian Road Directorate. Oslo.

5. DJURHUUS, O, B. SZALAI, J.M. GAMBARD, W. HALLER and P. TIELEMANS (1991). *Through Traffic In Small Towns: Safety And Environmental Aspects*. Routes-Roads. 1991. P1-44, AIPCR/PIARC, PARIS

6. IBI GROUP (1993) *Urban travel and sustainable development: the Canadian Experience*. Canada Mortgage and Housing Corporation.

7. COMMISSION OF THE EUROPEAN COMMUNITIES, DIRECTORATE-GENERAL FOR INFORMATION TECHNOLOGIES AND INDUSTRIES, AND TELECOMMUNICATIONS (DG XIII) (1993). *Transport Telematics 1993*; Annual Technical Report on RTD: Transport Telematics. Brussels.

8. HOLLOWAY, C.W. (1995). *Developing Priorities for Sustainable Transportation in Canada*. Report to Transport Canada, Environmental Stewardship Team. Envirotrans, Ottawa.

9. OFFICE OF THE GREATER TORONTO AREA (1992). *GTA 2021 - Infrastructure Report of the Provincial-Municipal Infrastructure Working Group*. Toronto.

10.   PISCHINGER, R. and others [Institut für Verbrennungskraftmaschinen und Thermodynamik, TU Graz], and SAMMER, G., and others [Institut für Straßen- und Verkehrswesen, TU Graz] (1995). *Tempo 30/50 in Graz.* Schriftenreihe der Institute für Straßen- und Verkehrswesen, Technische Universität Graz, Heft Nr. 21, 1995.

11.   HOPPE, KURT (1993). *The importance of public transport in a strongly ecological orientated traffic policy: the case of Bern.* In: ITE 1993 Compendium of Technical Papers (page 383-387).

      Gemeinderat der Stadt Bern: "Umwelt, Stadt und Verkehr; Kurzbericht zu den Verkehrskonzepten der Stadt Bern. 1982. Stadt Bern und Siemens AG: "Umwelt und Verkehr; Das neue Verkehrsrechnersystem in der Stadt Bern".

12.   DEPARTMENT OF TRANSPORT (1996*). Transport Policies and Programme Submissions for 1997-98.* Local Authority Circular 2/96, London.

13.   JARMAN, M (1994). *Costing the Benefits of the Oxford Transport Strategy. Transportation Planning Systems*, 1994 Vol. 2. No.2.

14.   OECD/ECMT (1995). *Urban travel and sustainable development.* OECD, Paris.

15.   DUBOIS-TAINE, G (1987). *P'TITAGOR Une méthodologie pour l'étude des traversées de petites agglomérations en application de principes de lisibilité de la route.* SETRA, Bagneux, France.

16.   ROAD DIRECTORATE OF DENMARK (1987*). Consequence evaluation of enviromentally adapted through road in Vinderup.* Road Data Laboratory, Report 52.

17.   WHEELER, A.H., ABBOT, P.G., GODFREY, N.S., PHILLIPS, S.M. and STAIT, R. (1997). *Traffic calming on major roads: the A47 trunk road at Thorney, Cambridgeshire.* TRL 238. Transport Research Laboratory, Crowthorne, U.K.

18.   WHEELER, A.H., ABBOT, P.G., GODFREY, LAWRENCE, D.J. and PHILLIPS,S.M. (1996). *Traffic calming on major roads: the A49 trunk road at Craven Arms, Shropshire.* TRL 212. Transport Research Laboratory, Crowthorne, U.K.

19.   LARSEN, S.N., LERSTANG, T., MYDSKE, P.K., RØE, P.G., SOLHEIM, T., STENSTADVOLD, M. and A. STRAND. *TP10 - A change of direction towards environmental policy? - The transportation planning in the ten largest urban areas in Norway: an evaluation of the process."* Samarbeidsrapport 3 (English Summary), Statens Vegvesten, Oslo.

20.   DEPARTMENT OF TRANSPORT (1994). *Design manual for roads and bridges.* HMSO, London.

CHAPTER V   ISSUES AND OPPORTUNITIES OF INTEGRATION

V.1. THE EVOLVING CONTEXT – FOUR PARADIGMS IN A CENTURY

Earlier portions of this report have related different traffic safety and environmental aspects to the focuses of different strategies and to the different interests of the actors in the field.   Behind these differences one can identify an evolving process that is linked to the development of car use and the problems of traffic.   This process can be described in several ways.   One way to characterise traffic safety strategy development is to use the "four paradigms in a century" approach.   The paradigms describe the evolution from controlling motorised carriage in the beginning of the 20th century, through mastering traffic situations and managing the traffic system, and then to managing the road transport system during the recent decades (1).   Looking at the interrelationship of traffic safety and environmental strategies, the shifts in focus that have taken place seem to determine the level of convergence or conflict.

In the first paradigm, or stage, the automobile is introduced into the transport system.   The main concern in this stage is managing the change in infrastructure and people's traffic behaviour to take account of the car.   Cars, buses and trucks are seen as a benefit, especially in the urban environment, as they supplant horse-drawn transport.

In the second stage, automobile becomes the dominant mode.   However, most drivers and other participants in traffic have relatively little experience with cars.   Accident numbers therefore increase dramatically.   Even though the accident numbers per capita may be low, car ownership not exceeding some 250 cars/1000 people, the relation of, for instance, fatalities to mileage is high.   The main traffic safety concerns are broad range campaigns to adapt people to manage traffic situations, for instance against speeding and drunk driving, and forming an efficient monitoring and vehicle inspection system.   Environmental aspects mainly concern direct nuisances and impediments to traffic flow.   At such a stage, there is little interaction between environmental and safety strategies.

In the third stage, as car mobility increases further, the initial traffic safety gains are counteracted by a much higher car ownership, i.e. 250 to 500 cars/1000 people, and accident numbers again rise. At this stage, environmental problems become more widespread, especially in urban areas where cars have taken the space of other modes of transportation.   Noise, exhaust pollution, barrier effects and conflicts with urban structure increase, as revealed in the following passage:

> "In many OECD Member countries, the number of road accident fatalities and injuries reached an all-time peak level around 1970.   During subsequent years, great progress was made in many countries in bringing down the number of casualties even with a further growth of mobility.   During the last decade, however, the decline in the number of casualties has slowed down in many countries.   Even in some countries, the numbers have started to rise again"(2).

In this stage, both the traffic safety and the environmental sectors place the emphasis on focused network action that is composed primarily by separate "black spot" actions. Traffic safety activity focuses on eliminating risk factors and environmental activity centres on significant nuisances. Though the strategies are similar, they are not co-ordinated and the actions are often in conflict. The emphasis is on new infrastructure construction. By-pass roads may, for instance, be built to improve city centre traffic conditions, but as a consequence surrounding housing areas may be fragmented. The need for integration begins to be most strongly felt when both traffic safety and environmental aspects are taken up as parts of a national transport policy.

In the fourth stage, as automobile ownership keeps growing, the dominance of car use comes increasingly into question and demands on traffic safety increase, especially for pedestrians and bicyclists. The traffic safety focus shifts to risk exposure and managing transport modes. The role of the road environment in accidents is emphasised, as is the role of the road as a part of the whole environment. The emphasis can be described by the following quotation regarding the characteristics of an intrinsically safe traffic system:

> "(It) has an infrastructure whose proper road design is adapted to the limitations of human capacity, a vehicle fitted with ways to simplify the task of the road user and constructed to protect human beings as effectively as possible, and a road user who is adequately educated, informed and, where necessary, controlled.
>
> As to infrastructure, the key to arrive at sustainable safety lies in the systematic and consistent application of three safety principles: the functional use of the road network, by preventing unintended use of each road, the homogeneous use, by preventing large differences in vehicle, speed, mass and direction of movement, the predictable use, thus preventing uncertainty amongst road users" (3).

In this stage, black spot action is only partially efficient because the main infrastructural problems have been remedied, at least regarding traffic safety aspects. Co-operation and integration are main themes in both sectors of safety and environment. There is an obvious basis for building integrated strategies, but also obvious problems in doing so, due to the wide range of partners and aspects involved. Another characteristic of this stage is the realisation that the cost of maintaining existing infrastructure is very high. The portion of funds that can be used for new infrastructure diminishes and the benefits of new construction show a declining rate of return because so much infrastructure is already in place.

The view on the socio-economic role of transport also undergoes a change in the fourth stage. Previously, it was seen as self-evident that the public budget was the way to finance infrastructure development, and the economic role of such development was held to be essential in all cases. But the emphasis shifts to considering the external as well as the internal costs of the different modes of transport, demanding that these costs be reflected in prices paid by the users, and that they are taken fully into account when considering the profitability of possible new projects.

Generally, there is a need to seek other ways than building new infrastructure to address problems. Decisions already taken, for instance on motorway network extensions, are reconsidered, and new methods of financing are sought for those projects that are retained.

The process summarised above is reflected in the evaluation of traffic safety and environmental aspects. The change from looking at individual drivers' and vehicles' problems to networks and vehicle fleets, from separate nuisances to a complex environment, demands an increasing sophistication in the methods and frameworks used.

In regard to traffic safety, the primary concern is reliably monitoring accident numbers and causes, then relating them to mileage and other factors. But monitoring needs to evolve into assessment of the efficiency of programmes and measures. Assessment can take place by asking such questions such as: Has the programme been implemented? Has it had the expected effect on safety? Have exogenous factors behaved in the expected way? If the answer to any of these questions is no, then one should ask why not? This approach presupposes detailed and representative data on road user behaviour and programme implementation. In the environmental sector, the emphasis has moved from measurement techniques for individual impacts to evaluation frameworks integrating a number of impacts.

The common focus of these approaches is the need to define clear and operational targets. Efficiency cannot be assessed unless it is related to a specific target to be achieved. Evaluation frameworks cannot function if the relationships between the targets for the different aspects are not identified. Otherwise, complexity very soon develops into confusion. The process of setting policy targets on the local, regional or national level leads to a new view of the sectors affected by the policies. Once the targets are expressed in comparable terms, a natural development is to question whether the instruments to realise these targets support or contradict one another.

V.2. DEVELOPING AN INTEGRATED STRATEGY

The call for integration extends to all modes of transport and from them to the structure of land use underlying transport demand. Such a broad field will, however, encompass many conflicts and competing objectives. Integrated strategies can serve to clarify the fundamental conflicts and priorities. Present strategy development emphasises concepts of sustainability, aiming at a positive interaction between transport modes and between transport and other infrastructure and land use. Some key objectives of this development are:

- Reasonability, equitable access for all user groups;
- Responsibility, often expressed in economic terms (user pays, polluter pays), but also in the relationship of different user groups to each other;
- Partnership, between authorities and organisations and between the public and private sectors;
- Involvement, of the public in strategy formulation.

Traffic safety and environmental objectives are given a position equal to the service level objectives of the infrastructure. But giving the objectives equal weight does not assure equal implementation, and broad strategies may end up in a strictly nominal integration, behind which the decisions on major infrastructure projects remain uninfluenced. Thus, the wider the viewpoint adopted in a strategy, the greater is the need for specific, operational methods of assessing how schemes and projects achieve strategic objectives. Public involvement increases the demand on the transparency of the assessment.

Based on a proposal for the contents of comprehensive traffic safety strategies (4), one can delineate some requirements for a successful strategy. It should build on a problem-oriented presentation and a clear description of the present situation. Based on a vision of the future, specific objectives for action should be identified and concrete targets set, focusing on groups and areas most exposed to risks. The strategy should provide operational instruments for evaluating impact, efficiency and cost efficiency, and for continuous monitoring of the results. Implementation should be organised with clearly specified responsibilities and duties of co-operation. Responsibilities and resources should be delegated as far as possible. Independent assessment should be provided.

These requirements parallel the characteristics that are referred to in the synthesis of Chapter IV for a successful process. The success of a strategy is to a large extent determined by the process that creates the strategy, but the strategy must naturally also have a valid objective and content.

V.3. ASPECTS OF DEVELOPMENT

There are several development trends concerning, in particular automobile technology, that are influencing future strategies and assessment. Intelligent transport systems are expected to reduce accident risks and increase routing efficiency, thus possibly also reducing fuel use and emissions. Engine and tyre development can reduce fuel use, exhausts and noise. On the other hand, as long as the increase in vehicle numbers and kilometrage continues, congestion, traffic energy use and emissions as a whole will also increase. As an example, traffic noise nuisance has grown regardless of the standards and vehicle emission limits introduced in the past 15 years, as describe in the following:

> "Data over the past 15 years do not show significant improvements in exposure to environmental noise, especially road traffic noise. Although exposure levels remained fairly stable at the beginning of the 1980s and action on "black spots" over 70 dB(A) have been successful [...] the proportion of the population exposed to levels above 65 dB(A) remained high and increases have been experienced by the end of the decade in many western European countries in the range of 55-65 dB(A), the so called grey zone, apparently as the result of fast growing volume of road traffic" (5).

In the foreseeable future, it is unlikely that technological change will eliminate the problems of transport and traffic. A continued decline in public infrastructure funding, combined with the increasing pressures on urban and especially metropolitan areas may instead deepen the severity of the problems encountered. This is occuring at a global level even though traffic growth in some developed countries has slowed, partly to a point where, for instance, the amount of fuel used for cars is stable or slightly declining. In this case, vehicle technology (fuel use efficiency) does keep up with kilometrage growth. But overall fuel consumption is also susceptible to changes in vehicle fleet composition, such as the increasing use of light trucks as personal automobiles in North America. Changes in noise emission measurement standards may bring a corresponding improvement of noise exposure. However, the overall state of the environmental impacts can well be described as in the following:

> "Increasing car travel is causing congestion, noise pollution and accidents in almost all cities large and small. People are becoming more dependent on cars and this has adverse effects on everyone, but especially on those without a car, who are becoming more and more isolated [...]. In most OECD countries the cost of congestion and accidents separately amount to about 2 percent of GDP, with noise and local air

pollution costing a further 0.5 to 1 per cent of GDP. Estimates of the long-term cost of CO_2 emissions to global warming vary between 1 and 10 per cent of GDP.

At the present time, most of the world's car fleet, and most of the local and global environmental problems created by cars in the cities, are found in developed countries. The transfer to cities in the developing countries of South America and South East Asia of the resource-hungry characteristics of Western urbanisation is an additional risk" (6) (see table V.1).

In the light of these problems and risks, developing functional integrated strategies may be an inescapable requirement for the future of the transport system. It is unlikely that separate actions first on, for instance, traffic safety, later on local environmental impacts and finally on the large-scale environmental impacts will, as a whole, lead to lasting improvement in situations of rapid traffic kilometrage growth. Here, too, separate action will most likely give rise to the kind of conflict exemplified by the third stage mentioned in section V.1.

It can be argued that integrated strategies will not be enough in such a situation. The fundamental need is to manage traffic demand development, which implies acting on the pattern, destinations and causes of travel. A sustainable transport system can evolve only when decisions take account of this responsibility. No strategy, however integrated it may be, is in itself sufficient to achieve this. But, considering that the pattern and causes of travel are dependent on, among other things, the functions and structure of land use, this argument can be interpreted as reinforcing the emphasis on land use, land use planning and urban planning as an essential factor in integrating the safety and environmental aspects of the transport system.

Table V.1. **Road transport indicators for OECD and other countries, 1990 and 2010**

	Light vehicles Totals			Heavy vehicles Totals		
	1990	**2010**	Δ	**1990**	**2010**	Δ
OECD countries						
Number of vehicles (millions)	469	672	+43%	16	25	+56%
Kilometres travelled (billions)	7,057	10,225	+45%	687	1,104	+61%
Weight of fuel used (megatonnes)	563	613	+9%	182	289	+59%
Non-OECD countries						
Number of vehicles (millions)	179	395	+121%	14	29	+107%
Kilometres travelled (billions)	2,380	5,239	+120%	647	1,311	+103%
Weight of fuel used (megatonnes)	167	284	+70%	142	288	+103%
All countries						
Number of vehicles (millions)	648	1,067	+65%	30	54	+80%
Kilometres travelled (billions)	9,437	15,464	+64%	1,334	2,415	+81%
Weight of fuel used (megatonnes)	730	897	+23%	324	577	+78%

Source: OECD/Environment Directorate

Travel demand development is also determined by social, economical and cultural factors. These are at most only indirectly influenced by the actions of, for instance, governments or road administrations. But among the factors clearly influenced by public action, planning and decision-making, the transport system in its land use context does have a central role, as do governmental decisions on prices through taxation. So, while there is a very real risk of an overall negative development, the task of the strategy is to act on precisely those factors that can be influenced, in order to achieve the best possible result in that context. A similar argument may hold for the other actors of the process, though, for instance, vehicle manufacturers have a more direct influence on the social and cultural factors of travel demand. Integrated strategy is a forum where these actors, too, deal with the public sphere and its possibilities.

V.4. A FIFTH PARADIGM

It was noted in section V.2 that a vision of the future is a prerequisite for integrated strategies. A vision is usually a mixture of what we expect to happen and what we would like to happen. In this section, some speculations are offered about the future context for larger-scale environmental and road safety integration. This is not a prediction, but a reflection on the following problem: Integration (or at least, co-ordination) works for limited actions on a large scale (e.g. national speed limits) or complex actions on a small scale (e.g. pedestrianisation of a historic core coupled with traffic calming measures and public transport improvements). "Getting it all together" for environment and road safety in a country or a large urban region will require a build-up of many localised components over a long period. But by the time enough components are in place, will the problem have evolved out of recognition? How can larger-scale environmental and road safety integration be steered and enabled in a way which takes into account the evolution of travel and freight transport demand discussed in section V.3?

This is by no means simply a question of the total quantity of vehicle-kilometres. There is a tension in social and economic trends which affects the nature of the transport system and its relationship to land use. Much of transport system development assumes the importance of accessibility, predictability and reliability in both passenger and freight transport. However, it is increasingly expensive to provide access to a wide variety of activities and goods for populations who live in lower density settlements. Yet tastes in OECD countries seem to be shifting towards a more spontaneous consumption of a high variety of activities and goods.

A transport system which serves such tastes will be more congested and chaotic in its performance than that serving a taste for relatively homogenous, stable sets of activities. In passenger transport, the dominant issue for individual behaviour is the difficulty of managing time, taking into account the complexities of the activities of those with whom activities are shared. Over the longer term, there are several possible reactions to this, some of which can be seen today: redensification in the form of a wider range of specialised settlements (e.g. retirement enclaves; youth-oriented neighbourhoods in older cities); greater integration of electronic communications in activity patterns, etc.

In freight transport, the theme of spontaneity is evident insofar as rapid distribution is needed to support a preference for manufacturing to order (just-in-time) over stockpiling. Ironically, this means that, in the case of freight, predictability and reliability in road transport is more important than ever, but it also means some transfer of investment from, for example, warehousing. Also, for consumer goods, the problem of final delivery to households has shifted increasingly to the consumer's own vehicle which may have to travel considerable distances to obtain a variety of goods.

These trends present both dilemmas and opportunities for the integration of environmental and road safety objectives. The institutional responses necessary to "get it all together" must be more dynamic than has historically occurred, especially around the safety issue. This means rapid feedback – a wider set of transparent indicators – in the future. If, as noted in V.2, traffic safety and environmental objectives are given a position equal to service level objectives of the infrastructure, then environmental and safety indicators must increasingly share the policy debate with the value of time or productivity lost in congestion.

Can we sketch out the origins and nature of an eventual "societal world view" which would value rapid and comprehensive feedback on the effects of incipient changes in the road transport system? In the beginning of this chapter the description of the evolution of the motorisation during this century, from the traffic safety perspective, was characterised as four paradigms, using the work of the OECD Expert Group on Road Safety Principles and Models (1).

From the environmental perspective a more or less similar evolution can be seen. At first one tries to repair the damages done by the system, its unwanted side-effects: houses with too high a noise load are made soundproof and insulated. In a second stage one tries to prevent the symptoms: noise barriers are built. Then one tries to change the system: e.g. rerouting major traffic flows. Finally comes the stage where the system is defined anew, from a new perspective of environment and sustainability.

The general description of the four paradigms shows a growing complexity. During the first period the car and the control of the individual car got the main attention. In the second period, this shifted to the traffic situation where different vehicles met. Then the whole traffic system became the dominating viewpoint. One step further brought the fourth paradigm where the transport system as a whole is being considered. A fifth paradigm logically follows this: the optimal result will not be found in the transport system alone, but one has to take other aspects into account.

The task for the coming years therefore may be characterised as the fifth paradigm, where the long term goals on environment and traffic safety will have to be balanced. An environmentally sustainable system should not use renewable resources at a higher rate than they are regenerated, or use non-renewable resources at a higher rate than substitutes are being developed. The present transport networks' carrying capacity for traffic, with respect to the flow of traffic as well as the impacts on the surroundings, is a limitation that should not be exceeded in such a system. Parallel to the demands for an environmentally sustainable system the goals for traffic safety within this fifth paradigm can be formulated as not causing irreversible injuries.

When one combines these characterisations, one arrives at a system which is both environmentally sustainable and intrinsically safe. This leads to integration of aspects, integration of institutions, integration of activities of different administrative levels, with differing geographical areas. The whole would become very complex. It must be recognised that it will be impossible to define the ideal end situation and the route to get there. A general view of this ideal will be needed, but operational goals have to be found closer by. It will therefore be necessary to focus more on the management of the process, and to monitor that process. In other words, new and flexible dimensions have to be found to divide the problem into manageable units, and from there coherent targets and problem situations have to be defined

Table V.2. **Paradigms of safety and environment (1)**

Aspects	Paradigms				
	I	**II**	**III**	**IV**	**V**
Period	1900 - 1925/35	1925/35 - 1965/70	1965/70 - 1980/85	1980/85 - present	present - 2010/20
	the car	the situation	the traffic system	the transport system	the transport system within the environment
Car availability	less than 25 per 1000 inhabitants	between 25 and 250	between 250 and 500	over 500	different cars for different tasks
Disciplines	law enforcement	car and road engineering, psychology	traffic engineering, traffic medicine, advanced statistics	advanced technology, systems analysis, sociology, communications	holistic systems approach, anthropology
'Unwanted' effects	collision	accident	crash and casualty	suffering and costs	system malfunction
Research	statistics: 'what'	the cause of accident: 'why'	the means: 'how'	multidimensional	co-operate and integrate
Organisational form	separate efforts based on trial and error	co-ordinated effort on voluntary basis	programmed efforts, authorised politically	decentralisation, local management	towards supranational, targeted actions and incentives for local, regional levels

There is thus a need to plan for a long term and with ambition: the goals are far-reaching and for the long run. In the long run the system should be intrinsically safe (in principle no persons killed or irreversibly injured), and sustainable. What is needed for success is a management philosophy that will help to implement large scale changes in society. Such a management philosophy has to be generally independent of institutional and cultural differences between organisations, regions and countries.

This can be realised with the aid of a hierarchical system of indicators. The hierarchies should start with definitions of what an intrinsically safe and sustainable transport system is, and then in two or three successive levels defined indicators that allow for planning and evaluation. Examples of these indicators are:

- speed of cars at non-separated crossings;
- proportion of non-fossil fuel;
- the proportion of pedestrians separated from car traffic..

Indicators can also take account of activities that have been reduced or are not possible in the present transport system, such as activities that could have been served by pedestrian trips. Private car use for ferrying children to school or other comparable activities can indicate deficiencies in bicycle and pedestrian safety.

The indicators also have to be suitable for setting annual goals and evaluating performance. But one also needs indicators on vital aspects of the processes to reach the goals. These indicators concern, among other things, the activities of the different actors (police, local authorities) and focus on, for instance, competence, motivation and co-operation. The indicators should ideally be generated by whatever agency can most effectively, independently and transparently monitor the performance of the road system on all three types of objectives – service level, safety and environmental quality. In the future context, several levels of control might be made accountable on this wider set of indicators, while still allowing much flexibility in the choice of mitigating interventions by the different levels of government, industry, etc.

Land use policies can be instrumental in reaching a balance between accessibility and environmental protection. Land use policies already influence to a great extent the ranges within which later environmental and traffic safety policies can be developed. In Section II.5 a number of key elements for such a policy were noted.

V.5. REFERENCES

1.   OECD. ROAD TRANSPORT RESEARCH (1997). *Road Safety Principles and Models.* OECD, Paris.

2.   OECD. ROAD TRANSPORT RESEARCH (1994). *Targeted Road Safety Programmes.* OECD, Paris.

3.   PIARC (1996). *Road accidents, a world-wide problem that can be tackled successfully.* PIARC Committee on Road Safety. Paris.

4.   RUMAR, K. (1996). *De nordiska trafiksäkerhetsprogrammens roll i trafiksäkerhetsarbetet / The role of the Nordic traffic safety programs in traffic safety action*; Via Nordica, Papers of the 17. Congress of the Nordic Road Federation, Bergen.

5.   COMMISSION OF THE EUROPEAN COMMUNITIES (1996). *Future Noise Policy*; European Commission Green Paper, COM(96) 540 final, Luxembourg.

6.   OECD/ECMT (1995). *Urban Travel and Sustainable Development.* OECD, Paris.

CHAPTER VI   CONCLUSIONS AND RECOMMENDATIONS

VI.1. THE ADVANTAGES OF INTEGRATED STRATEGY

The environmental and traffic safety aspects of the transport system are closely related, especially in the perspective of human health and well-being. In current practice, there are few cases showing a conscious effort to treat safety and environmental objectives within an integrated framework, where gains or trade-offs between the two are made explicit. More common is co-ordination, a simultaneous consideration of the two issues. But often, they are still taken separately.

There is therefore a risk that action to improve one will be at the expense of the other. This is particularly a potential problem when, for example, traffic re-distribution or traffic calming measures are being used. Lack of integration appears to be largely because the benefits and disbenefits are not obvious; institutions and actors are organised with their own specialist interests, responsibilities and targets. The practitioners do not share a common culture on safety and environmental problems. Decision makers and the public lack full knowledge of impacts and are reluctant to change their priorities for action.

There are some clear advantages to the integration of road safety and environment protection:

- An increase of the benefits in case of an action contributing both to the reduction of accidents and of environmental disturbance. An action seen to have insufficient benefits in relation to its costs for one of the sectors, can improve its standing if the benefits for the other sector are realised – the benefits increase, while the cost remains the same. Actions can also gain better public acceptance, if their implications are shown for the larger context.

- A better optimisation if an action contributes positively to one sector but negatively to the other. In this case, as the framework of the decision is enlarged, it is possible to detect actions which deteriorate the conditions of the whole system instead of improving it. Integration is necessary to find complementary action in order to correct the negative effect. If we encourage bicycling in cities in order to influence modal split and reduce pollution, we have to provide safe conditions for the bicyclists through appropriate safety measures, otherwise the number of injuries will increase due to the cyclists' vulnerability.

The problems of integration lie in the expansion of the sphere of action and the increasing number of criteria. The decision process is more complicated and has to look at a broader scale of impacts. Long-term effects are introduced and the question of process interaction needs to be dealt with on a more sophisticated level as the system expands.

VI.2. INSTITUTIONS AND PLANS

In an integrated strategy, a broad field of goals is systematically translated into a set of mutually reinforcing packages of measures. The main requirement of integration is that the actors involved join in a co-operative process with clearly specified, concrete objectives.

If the responsibility for infrastructure development is divided between many administrations, institutional reform or creation of new structures connecting the sectors to each other can be one precondition for developing an integrated strategy. But the essence of integration is rarely achieved through building new administrations or by defining new levels of planning. The focus is rather on improving the manner in which different actors recognise the need for co-operation and their readiness to implement it. The starting point is in improving communication and the dialogue between the different public administrations and the competent authorities.

There is also a need to strengthen the dialogue with industry and the public, mobilising the social and economic forces, using market incentives rather than regulation. The technical progress achieved in developing new energy sources, new materials for vehicle construction, telematics for vehicle guidance and freight transport logistics should be put into use to serve the objectives of safety and environmental protection.

The contents of strategy are different on the national, regional and local level, but the common need on these levels is a firm connection to land use planning, urban planning and design. Transport system development has a direct influence on urban structure, on the relative competitiveness of locations as well as transport modes. Planning for transport, especially road and street network improvement, is a part of urban planning.

The location of activities and the physical context given them are an essential factor in how travel demand develops and what kind of transport can serve that demand. Walking and cycling are especially sensitive to the environmental quality and safety of the route, public transport to how efficiently stops and terminals serve their catchment areas, how regular and frequent the service is, etc. Some groups, such as children and older people, can be more sensitive to the effects of traffic than others, and should be given special consideration.

Long-term strategy, especially on the level of Government policy, presupposes a high level of integration. National transport policy needs to be discussed at the highest level possible and with a sufficient time scale, say 15 years.

The implementation of long-term strategies is usually defined in administrative action programmes for the shorter term, 4 to 10 years. The elaboration of such action programs is a crucial step for integrated strategy, because it is at this stage that the cross-connections between different actions and the needs for co-operation can be clearly identified. The interaction with land use planning focuses on regional development plans and master plans.

Short-term action, that is, implementation of specific projects and measures, is naturally divided according to the respective responsibilities of the actors involved. Here, the concept of integration essentially implies that the actors, when implementing their measures, should act in contact with each other and co-ordinating the measures as necessary.

VI.3. TOWARDS INTEGRATIVE STRATEGIES

For a strategy, both visions of the future and a clear view of the present and its problems are needed. Visions are necessary to clarify what really should be achieved. They also engage the imagination and creativity. In the form of alternative scenarios, visions can express the aims of the different actors involved.

While the scenarios of different actors can show a large variation, the view of the present, and of what the problems are, should be shared by the actors. The problem formulation should be carefully considered, because it determines what kinds of measures are looked at. Awareness of this leads the actors to put long-term considerations at the forefront and to look for measures that integrate, at the outset, safety and environmental protection, rather than corrective measures that may be necessary to limit damages, but not sufficient to reverse trends.

To be successful, a strategy needs firm objectives. Objectives that can be expressed as quantified targets, say regarding the reduction of carbon dioxide emissions expected of the transport sector in a given period, have a prominent role, but not all concerns can be quantified in this manner. Beauty, quality of life or protection of biodiversity should also be given specific expression, but there are not always the tools to do so. One way is to set, instead, targets for the actions to improve performance, for instance for training professionals, including in the curriculum of engineers the integration of environmental and road safety aspects, or improving vehicle inspection efficiency. Another is to ask the public to evaluate what has been done and what needs to be done.

A strategy needs to be flexible in regard of implementation. Organisations change, funding changes and new schemes arise, and the strategy should adapt itself to these changes. This emphasises the process nature of the strategy; it is not a document to be adopted once and for all, but a process where the actors involved regularly meet to review how the objectives have been implemented and what the changes mean for future implementation. Some key factors of the process contributing to the success of integration are:

- asking leading questions about safety and environmental goals at the start,
- an appropriate choice of public involvement,
- detection of instabilities, issues with special political or other connotations,
- taking account of the paradoxes in what people will accept,
- due consideration for points of no return, particularly concerning car-dependence,
- articulating comprehensive packages of measures for which the longer-term safety and environment payoffs are made explicit,
- identifying the gainers and losers from particular decisions,
- making it possible to learn from past failures as well as successes.

VI.4. RECOMMENDATIONS

From country to country, the differences on how to implement integration can be considerable, but some recommendations seem evident:

In any policy and scheme development, transparency towards all actors, institutions and citizens involved is a prime concern. The consequences in regard of safety and environment should always be taken into account. In developing environmental policy, the safety aspects should be made explicit; in safety policy, the environmental aspects. A common set of indicators should be used.

The key indicators most reflective of the sustainability of the transport system are modal split, motor vehicle kilometrage and energy use. An overall increase in motor vehicle use or in vehicle kilometrage indicates a non-sustainable trend. However, such global indicators are insufficient to evaluate the efficiency of measures to reduce dependency on motor vehicles: more detailed indicators are needed which take into account the societal benefits and productivity of motorised travel, which are not constant on a vehicle-kilometre basis. Examples of indicators useful in such a system are:

- speed of cars at non-separated crossings;
- proportion of transport not dependent on use of fossil fuels;
- the proportion of pedestrians separated from car traffic.

Indicators on vital aspects of the processes to reach the goals are also needed. These indicators concern the activities of the different actors and focus on competence, motivation and co-operation. Technological, economic and regulative action should be considered as an entire package. To achieve more than a marginal impact on present trends, all of these have to be used.

Environmental impact assessment has developed as a powerful tool to evaluate the environmental aspects of a project or policy at an early stage, while road safety audits are gaining increasing importance in assessing implementation of safety. Developing EIA to ensure that a sufficient range of environmental concerns are taken into account in implementation and further developing the use of the safety audit technique to serve early stages of planning may form an efficient way of bringing these concerns together in the planning process.

Project objectives should include the manner of dealing with such matters as severance and visual intrusion in urban areas, risks to the cultural heritage, fragmentation of natural areas, and water pollution. At present, these are generally seen as external constraints. This perception may lead to serious conflicts in a late stage of planning, because the project can not comply with the constraints, if it has not taken account of the goals such constraints relate to. Especially when large scale infrastructure schemes or wide-ranging regulatory or economic action is proposed, the risks of irreversible change should be carefully considered.

One should be aware that some groups of measures show clearly different relationships to the theme of integration:

- Measures such as speed reduction and improved enforcement lead to overall safety and environmental quality improvement, regardless of the context of their development.

- Others, such as traffic management and redistribution, can cause conflicts, if they are implemented without consideration of all aspects and also impacts on other areas and parts of the transport network.

- But there are also measures essential to either safety or environmental quality with little impact on other aspects. For safety, such are, for instance, measures against drinking before driving, for environment, reduction of vehicle exhaust pollutants. Resources to implement these measures need to be available regardless of the intents of integration.

As a first step, each organisation responsible for a sector should undertake an impact evaluation study in the other sector. This implies a common set of indicators and an exchange of knowledge between the two sectors. At a later stage, the aim is designing an ecological and safe system of transport instead of corrective actions. It demands a higher level of integration between the parties and a new way to organise the process.

VI.5. NEEDS FOR RESEARCH

There are still barriers between the sectors, which can only be reduced by a concerted research effort. A special need is developing tools for testing and assessing policies, based on scientific knowledge regarding safety, environmental pollution and noise. There is a role for carefully designed pilot schemes, to examine both the implementation process and the technical effects of measures chosen.

The models for predicting accidents, pollutant emissions and noise should have a common basis in vehicle and traffic flow data. Models need to be developed for use both on the micro level, in evaluating the impacts of changes in a road or area, and on the macro level, in forecasting the long-term effects of changes in vehicle fleet composition or traffic flows. It is also important that data bases as well as models take better account of all groups of pedestrians and bicyclists. Health effects, especially of atmospheric pollutants, need further research.

Further research is needed on the environmental impacts of safety schemes and on the safety impacts of environmental schemes. Professional research is also needed into the social and societal impacts of such schemes.

Considering the planning and design process, further research is needed on process management, on preparing and making decisions, and to find new ways to order complex tasks into manageable components. Better evaluation methodology and frameworks, allowing taking multiple relevant dimensions or criteria into account in a transparent manner, are also needed.

Research is also needed on efficient ways to influence the members of the public to promote safe and environmentally adapted choices in making travel decisions and implementing them. This is an ethical aspect, which goes beyond the scope of the transport process itself.

In regard of policies and measures, the main contemporary questions are:

- how to influence transport demand,
- how to increase the role of non-motorised traffic and, where appropriate, public transport in transport system implementation,
- finding the packages of measures relevant for entire regions surrounding large urban areas,
- responding to the process of rapid motorisation in developing economies.

There as yet few measures dealing successfully with these four underlying issues, or which take them up with a concern for both safety and environment. While those approaches that have shown some measure of success underline the importance of tailoring polices and strategies to the concrete situation of each country and locality, they also demonstrate the importance of the international exchange of know-how concerning the methods and measures which fit into a given situation. OECD research is one channel for such exchange.

The work of this Group has revealed a modest, but growing, awareness of the need to make the safety and environmental balance-sheets coherent and accessible, as a normal part of road transport planning. In some cases, even posing the question served to raise that awareness. Further OECD studies could focus on specific applications of the approaches recommended in this report to one or more of those four underlying issues.

LIST OF PARTICIPANTS

Chairmen : Mr A. HH Jansson (Finland) and Mr S. Lassarre (France)

Australia   Mr Leo DOBES
(Bureau of Transport and
Communications Economics)

Austria   Mr Hermann KNOFLACHER
(Technical University of Vienna)   Mr Thomas MACOUN

Canada   Mr Martin LEE-GOSSELIN
(Département d'Aménagement de
l'Université Laval, Québec)

Denmark   Mr Hans BENDTSEN
(Danish Road Directorate)

Finland   Mr Anders HH JANSSON
(FinnRa)

France   Mr Jacques LAMBERT
(INRETS)   Mr Sylvain LASSARRE

Germany   Mr Günter SABOW
(DEKRA)

Hungary   Mrs Agnes MESZAROS-KIS
(KTI)   Mr Boldizsar VASARHELYI

Italy   Mr Antonio TRAMONTIN
(University of Calgliari and
ANAS)

Japan   Mr Masakazu NAKAGAWA
(National Police Agency)

Netherlands   Mr Frank POPPE
(SVOW)

Norway   Mrs Anne Underthun MARSTEIN
(Public Road Administration)

Sweden
(National Road Administration)

Mr Roger JOHANSSON

Mr Svante NORDLANDER

Switzerland
(Bureau suisse de prévention des accidents)

Mr Roland ALLENBACH

United Kingdom
(TRL on behalf of the Department of Transport)

Mr Archie MACKIE

OECD/ENV

Mr Peter WIEDERKEHR

OECD/RTR

Mr Burkhard HORN

Mr Claude MORIN

Ms Véronique FEYPELL

MAIN SALES OUTLETS OF OECD PUBLICATIONS
PRINCIPAUX POINTS DE VENTE DES PUBLICATIONS DE L'OCDE

AUSTRALIA – AUSTRALIE
D.A. Information Services
648 Whitehorse Road, P.O.B 163
Mitcham, Victoria 3132   Tel. (03) 9210.7777
                             Fax: (03) 9210.7788

AUSTRIA – AUTRICHE
Gerold & Co.
Graben 31
Wien I   Tel. (0222) 533.50.14
                             Fax: (0222) 512.47.31.29

BELGIUM – BELGIQUE
Jean De Lannoy
Avenue du Roi, Koningslaan 202
B-1060 Bruxelles   Tel. (02) 538.51.69/538.08.41
                             Fax: (02) 538.08.41

CANADA
Renouf Publishing Company Ltd.
5369 Canotek Road
Unit 1
Ottawa, Ont. K1J 9J3   Tel. (613) 745.2665
                             Fax: (613) 745.7660

Stores:
71 1/2 Sparks Street
Ottawa, Ont. K1P 5R1   Tel. (613) 238.8985
                             Fax: (613) 238.6041

12 Adelaide Street West
Toronto, QN M5H 1L6   Tel. (416) 363.3171
                             Fax: (416) 363.5963

Les Éditions La Liberté Inc.
3020 Chemin Sainte-Foy
Sainte-Foy, PQ G1X 3V6   Tel. (418) 658.3763
                             Fax: (418) 658.3763

Federal Publications Inc.
165 University Avenue, Suite 701
Toronto, ON M5H 3B8   Tel. (416) 860.1611
                             Fax: (416) 860.1608

Les Publications Fédérales
1185 Université
Montréal, QC H3B 3A7   Tel. (514) 954.1633
                             Fax: (514) 954.1635

CHINA – CHINE
Book Dept., China National Publications
Import and Export Corporation (CNPIEC)
16 Gongti E. Road, Chaoyang District
Beijing 100020   Tel. (10) 6506-6688 Ext. 8402
                             (10) 6506-3101

CHINESE TAIPEI – TAIPEI CHINOIS
Good Faith Worldwide Int'l. Co. Ltd.
9th Floor, No. 118, Sec. 2
Chung Hsiao E. Road
Taipei   Tel. (02) 391.7396/391.7397
                             Fax: (02) 394.9176

**CZECH REPUBLIC –
RÉPUBLIQUE TCHÈQUE**
National Information Centre
NIS – prodejna
Konviktská 5
Praha 1 – 113 57   Tel. (02) 24.23.09.07
                             Fax: (02) 24.22.94.33
E-mail: nkposp@dec.niz.cz
Internet: http://www.nis.cz

DENMARK – DANEMARK
Munksgaard Book and Subscription Service
35, Nørre Søgade, P.O. Box 2148
DK-1016 København K   Tel. (33) 12.85.70
                             Fax: (33) 12.93.87

J. H. Schultz Information A/S,
Herstedvang 12,
DK – 2620 Albertslung   Tel. 43 63 23 00
                             Fax: 43 63 19 69

Internet: s-info@inet.uni-c.dk

EGYPT – ÉGYPTE
The Middle East Observer
41 Sherif Street
Cairo   Tel. (2) 392.6919
                             Fax: (2) 360.6804

FINLAND – FINLANDE
Akateeminen Kirjakauppa
Keskuskatu 1, P.O. Box 128
00100 Helsinki

Subscription Services/Agence d'abonnements :
P.O. Box 23
00100 Helsinki   Tel. (358) 9.121.4403
                             Fax: (358) 9.121.4450

*FRANCE
OECD/OCDE
Mail Orders/Commandes par correspondance :
2, rue André-Pascal
75775 Paris Cedex 16   Tel. 33 (0)1.45.24.82.00
                        Fax: 33 (0)1.49.10.42.76
                             Telex: 640048 OCDE
Internet: Compte.PUBSINQ@oecd.org

Orders via Minitel, France only/
Commandes par Minitel, France exclusivement :
36 15 OCDE

OECD Bookshop/Librairie de l'OCDE :
33, rue Octave-Feuillet
75016 Paris   Tel. 33 (0)1.45.24.81.81
                        33 (0)1.45.24.81.67

Dawson
B.P. 40
91121 Palaiseau Cedex   Tel. 01.89.10.47.00
                             Fax: 01.64.54.83.26

Documentation Française
29, quai Voltaire
75007 Paris   Tel. 01.40.15.70.00

Economica
49, rue Héricart
75015 Paris   Tel. 01.45.78.12.92
                             Fax: 01.45.75.05.67

Gibert Jeune (Droit-Économie)
6, place Saint-Michel
75006 Paris   Tel. 01.43.25.91.19

Librairie du Commerce International
10, avenue d'Iéna
75016 Paris   Tel. 01.40.73.34.60

Librairie Dunod
Université Paris-Dauphine
Place du Maréchal-de-Lattre-de-Tassigny
75016 Paris   Tel. 01.44.05.40.13

Librairie Lavoisier
11, rue Lavoisier
75008 Paris   Tel. 01.42.65.39.95

Librairie des Sciences Politiques
30, rue Saint-Guillaume
75007 Paris   Tel. 01.45.48.36.02

P.U.F.
49, boulevard Saint-Michel
75005 Paris   Tel. 01.43.25.83.40

Librairie de l'Université
12a, rue Nazareth
13100 Aix-en-Provence   Tel. 04.42.26.18.08

Documentation Française
165, rue Garibaldi
69003 Lyon   Tel. 04.78.63.32.23

Librairie Decitre
29, place Bellecour
69002 Lyon   Tel. 04.72.40.54.54

Librairie Sauramps
Le Triangle
34967 Montpellier Cedex 2   Tel. 04.67.58.85.15
                             Fax: 04.67.58.27.36

A la Sorbonne Actual
23, rue de l'Hôtel-des-Postes
06000 Nice   Tel. 04.93.13.77.75
                             Fax: 04.93.80.75.69

GERMANY – ALLEMAGNE
OECD Bonn Centre
August-Bebel-Allee 6
D-53175 Bonn   Tel. (0228) 959.120
                             Fax: (0228) 959.12.17

GREECE – GRÈCE
Librairie Kauffmann
Stadiou 28
10564 Athens   Tel. (01) 32.55.321
                             Fax: (01) 32.30.320

HONG-KONG
Swindon Book Co. Ltd.
Astoria Bldg. 3F
34 Ashley Road, Tsimshatsui
Kowloon, Hong Kong   Tel. 2376.2062
                             Fax: 2376.0685

HUNGARY – HONGRIE
Euro Info Service
Margitsziget, Európa Ház
1138 Budapest   Tel. (1) 111.60.61
                             Fax: (1) 302.50.35
E-mail: euroinfo@mail.matav.hu
Internet: http://www.euroinfo.hu//index.html

ICELAND – ISLANDE
Mál og Menning
Laugavegi 18, Pósthólf 392
121 Reykjavik   Tel. (1) 552.4240
                             Fax: (1) 562.3523

INDIA – INDE
Oxford Book and Stationery Co.
Scindia House
New Delhi 110001   Tel. (11) 331.5896/5308
                             Fax: (11) 332.2639
E-mail: oxford.publ@axcess.net.in

17 Park Street
Calcutta 700016   Tel. 240832

INDONESIA – INDONÉSIE
Pdii-Lipi
P.O. Box 4298
Jakarta 12042   Tel. (21) 573.34.67
                             Fax: (21) 573.34.67

IRELAND – IRLANDE
Government Supplies Agency
Publications Section
4/5 Harcourt Road
Dublin 2   Tel. 661.31.11
                             Fax: 475.27.60

ISRAEL – ISRAËL
Praedicta
5 Shatner Street
P.O. Box 34030
Jerusalem 91430   Tel. (2) 652.84.90/1/2
                             Fax: (2) 652.84.93

R.O.Y. International
P.O. Box 13056
Tel Aviv 61130   Tel. (3) 546 1423
                             Fax: (3) 546 1442
E-mail: royil@netvision.net.il

Palestinian Authority/Middle East:
INDEX Information Services
P.O.B. 19502
Jerusalem   Tel. (2) 627.16.34
                             Fax: (2) 627.12.19

ITALY – ITALIE
Libreria Commissionaria Sansoni
Via Duca di Calabria, 1/1
50125 Firenze   Tel. (055) 64.54.15
                             Fax: (055) 64.12.57
E-mail: licosa@ftbcc.it

Via Bartolini 29
20155 Milano   Tel. (02) 36.50.83

Editrice e Libreria Herder
Piazza Montecitorio 120
00186 Roma   Tel. 679.46.28
                             Fax: 678.47.51

Libreria Hoepli
Via Hoepli 5
20121 Milano   Tel. (02) 86.54.46
                             Fax: (02) 805.28.86

Libreria Scientifica
Dott. Lucio de Biasio 'Aeiou'
Via Coronelli, 6
20146 Milano   Tel. (02) 48.95.45.52
Fax: (02) 48.95.45.48

JAPAN – JAPON
OECD Tokyo Centre
Landic Akasaka Building
2-3-4 Akasaka, Minato-ku
Tokyo 107   Tel. (81.3) 3586.2016
Fax: (81.3) 3584.7929

KOREA – CORÉE
Kyobo Book Centre Co. Ltd.
P.O. Box 1658, Kwang Hwa Moon
Seoul   Tel. 730.78.91
Fax: 735.00.30

MALAYSIA – MALAISIE
University of Malaya Bookshop
University of Malaya
P.O. Box 1127, Jalan Pantai Baru
59700 Kuala Lumpur
Malaysia   Tel. 756.5000/756.5425
Fax: 756.3246

MEXICO – MEXIQUE
OECD Mexico Centre
Edificio INFOTEC
Av. San Fernando no. 37
Col. Toriello Guerra
Tlalpan C.P. 14050
Mexico D.F.   Tel. (525) 528.10.38
Fax: (525) 606.13.07
E-mail: ocde@rtn.net.mx

NETHERLANDS – PAYS-BAS
SDU Uitgeverij Plantijnstraat
Externe Fondsen
Postbus 20014
2500 EA's-Gravenhage   Tel. (070) 37.89.880
Voor bestellingen: Fax: (070) 34.75.778

Subscription Agency/   Agence d'abonnements :
SWETS & ZEITLINGER BV
Heereweg 347B
P.O. Box 830
2160 SZ Lisse   Tel. 252.435.111
Fax: 252.415.888

**NEW ZEALAND –
NOUVELLE-ZÉLANDE**
GPLegislation Services
P.O. Box 12418
Thorndon, Wellington   Tel. (04) 496.5655
Fax: (04) 496.5698

NORWAY – NORVÈGE
NIC INFO A/S
Ostensjoveien 18
P.O. Box 6512 Etterstad
0606 Oslo   Tel. (22) 97.45.00
Fax: (22) 97.45.45

PAKISTAN
Mirza Book Agency
65 Shahrah Quaid-E-Azam
Lahore 54000   Tel. (42) 735.36.01
Fax: (42) 576.37.14

PHILIPPINE – PHILIPPINES
International Booksource Center Inc.
Rm 179/920 Cityland 10 Condo Tower 2
HV dela Costa Ext cor Valero St.
Makati Metro Manila   Tel. (632) 817 9676
Fax: (632) 817 1741

POLAND – POLOGNE
Ars Polona
00-950 Warszawa
Krakowskie Prezdmiescie 7   Tel. (22) 264760
Fax: (22) 265334

PORTUGAL
Livraria Portugal
Rua do Carmo 70-74
Apart. 2681
1200 Lisboa   Tel. (01) 347.49.82/5
Fax: (01) 347.02.64

SINGAPORE – SINGAPOUR
Ashgate Publishing
Asia Pacific Pte. Ltd
Golden Wheel Building, 04-03
41, Kallang Pudding Road
Singapore 349316   Tel. 741.5166
Fax: 742.9356

SPAIN – ESPAGNE
Mundi-Prensa Libros S.A.
Castelló 37, Apartado 1223
Madrid 28001   Tel. (91) 431.33.99
Fax: (91) 575.39.98
E-mail: mundiprensa@tsai.es
Internet: http://www.mundiprensa.es

Mundi-Prensa Barcelona
Consell de Cent No. 391
08009 – Barcelona   Tel. (93) 488.34.92
Fax: (93) 487.76.59

Libreria de la Generalitat
Palau Moja
Rambla dels Estudis, 118
08002 – Barcelona
(Suscripciones) Tel. (93) 318.80.12
(Publicaciones) Tel. (93) 302.67.23
Fax: (93) 412.18.54

SRI LANKA
Centre for Policy Research
c/o Colombo Agencies Ltd.
No. 300-304, Galle Road
Colombo 3   Tel. (1) 574240, 573551-2
Fax: (1) 575394, 510711

SWEDEN – SUÈDE
CE Fritzes AB
S–106 47 Stockholm   Tel. (08) 690.90.90
Fax: (08) 20.50.21

For electronic publications only/
Publications électroniques seulement
STATISTICS SWEDEN
Informationsservice
S-115 81 Stockholm   Tel. 8 783 5066
Fax: 8 783 4045

Subscription Agency/Agence d'abonnements :
Wennergren-Williams Info AB
P.O. Box 1305
171 25 Solna   Tel. (08) 705.97.50
Fax: (08) 27.00.71

Liber distribution
International organizations
Fagerstagatan 21
S-163 52 Spanga

SWITZERLAND – SUISSE
Maditec S.A. (Books and Periodicals/Livres
et périodiques)
Chemin des Palettes 4
Case postale 266
1020 Renens VD 1   Tel. (021) 635.08.65
Fax: (021) 635.07.80

Librairie Payot S.A.
4, place Pépinet
CP 3212
1002 Lausanne   Tel. (021) 320.25.11
Fax: (021) 320.25.14

Librairie Unilivres
6, rue de Candolle
1205 Genève   Tel. (022) 320.26.23
Fax: (022) 329.73.18

Subscription Agency/Agence d'abonnements :
Dynapresse Marketing S.A.
38, avenue Vibert
1227 Carouge   Tel. (022) 308.08.70
Fax: (022) 308.07.99

See also – Voir aussi :
OECD Bonn Centre
August-Bebel-Allee 6
D-53175 Bonn (Germany)   Tel. (0228) 959.120
Fax: (0228) 959.12.17

THAILAND – THAÏLANDE
Suksit Siam Co. Ltd.
113, 115 Fuang Nakhon Rd.
Opp. Wat Rajbopith
Bangkok 10200   Tel. (662) 225.9531/2
Fax: (662) 222.5188

**TRINIDAD & TOBAGO, CARIBBEAN
TRINITÉ-ET-TOBAGO, CARAÏBES**
Systematics Studies Limited
9 Watts Street
Curepe
Trinidad & Tobago, W.I.   Tel. (1809) 645.3475
Fax: (1809) 662.5654
E-mail: tobe@trinidad.net

TUNISIA – TUNISIE
Grande Librairie Spécialisée
Fendri Ali
Avenue Haffouz Imm El-Intilaka
Bloc B 1 Sfax 3000   Tel. (216-4) 296 855
Fax: (216-4) 298.270

TURKEY – TURQUIE
Kültür Yayinlari Is-Türk Ltd.
Atatürk Bulvari No. 191/Kat 13
06684 Kavaklidere/Ankara   Tel. (312) 428.11.40 Ext. 2458
Fax : (312) 417.24.90
Dolmabahce Cad. No. 29
Besiktas/Istanbul   Tel. (212) 260 7188

UNITED KINGDOM – ROYAUME-UNI
The Stationery Office Ltd.
Postal orders only:
P.O. Box 276, London SW8 5DT
Gen. enquiries   Tel. (171) 873 0011
Fax: (171) 873 8463

The Stationery Office Ltd.
Postal orders only:
49 High Holborn, London WC1V 6HB
Branches at: Belfast, Birmingham, Bristol,
Edinburgh, Manchester

UNITED STATES – ÉTATS-UNIS
OECD Washington Center
2001 L Street N.W., Suite 650
Washington, D.C. 20036-4922 Tel. (202) 785.6323
Fax: (202) 785.0350
Internet: washcont@oecd.org

Subscriptions to OECD periodicals may also be
placed through main subscription agencies.

Les abonnements aux publications périodiques de
l'OCDE peuvent être souscrits auprès des
principales agences d'abonnement.

Orders and inquiries from countries where Distribu-
tors have not yet been appointed should be sent to:
OECD Publications, 2, rue André-Pascal, 75775
Paris Cedex 16, France.

Les commandes provenant de pays où l'OCDE n'a
pas encore désigné de distributeur peuvent être
adressées aux Éditions de l'OCDE, 2, rue André-
Pascal, 75775 Paris Cedex 16, France.

12-1996

OECD PUBLICATIONS, 2, rue André-Pascal, 75775 PARIS CÉDEX 16
PRINTED IN FRANCE
(77 97 06 1 P) ISBN 92-64-15664-X – No. 49771 1997